D1650016

Big
Potential

ALSO BY SHAWN ACHOR

The Happiness Advantage

Before Happiness

The Ripples Effect

The Orange Frog

Big Potential

Five Secrets of Reaching Higher by Powering Those Around You

Shawn Achor

1 3 5 7 9 10 8 6 4 2

Virgin Books, an imprint of Ebury Publishing,
20 Vauxhall Bridge Road,
London SW1V 2SA

Virgin Books is part of the Penguin Random House group of companies
whose addresses can be found at global.penguinrandomhouse.com

Penguin
Random House
UK

Copyright © Shawn Achor 2018

Shawn Achor has asserted his right to be identified as the author of this
Work in accordance with the Copyright, Designs and Patents Act 1988

First published in the United Kingdom by Virgin Books in 2018
First published in the United States by Currency in 2018

www.penguin.co.uk

A CIP catalogue record for this book is available from the British Library

ISBN 9780753552216

Printed and bound in Great Britain by Clays Ltd, St Ives PLC

Penguin Random House is committed to a sustainable future for our
business, our readers and our planet. This book is made from Forest
Stewardship Council® certified paper.

For Michelle and Leo,

two brilliant lights of joy who daily remind me

love is the only way

to see our full potential

CONTENTS

○ ○ ○ ○ ○

PART I: THE BIG PROBLEM WITH SMALL POTENTIAL

PART II: THE SEEDS OF BIG POTENTIAL

Big
Potential

THE
BIG PROBLEM
WITH
SMALL
POTENTIAL

CHAPTER 1

THE POWER OF HIDDEN CONNECTIONS

The creation of a thousand forests is in one acorn.
—RALPH WALDO EMERSON

THE MIRACLE OF THE MANGROVES

When dusk slowly crept upon a mangrove forest lining a river deep in a jungle in Southeast Asia, a biologist far from his home in Washington State looked out over the lush, alien landscape lining the snake-infested waters. While drifting slowly in his boat, Professor Hugh Smith surely heard the calls of the nocturnal creatures uncoiling from their dens or taking flight from their nests and beginning their nightly hunts. I can envision how the water must have shimmered under the light from the stars, unspoiled by the light pollution that existed in the remote cities. What happened next on that humid day in 1935 is part of recorded academic history. Smith looked up at one of the mangrove trees, and suddenly the entire canopy glowed as if a lightning bolt had shot out from the tree instead of striking it. Then all went dark, leaving a burned image on his vision.

Then lightning, as it sometimes does, struck twice.

The entire tree glowed again, then went entirely dark again twice in three seconds.[1] Then, in a reality-bending moment, all of the trees along the riverbank suddenly glowed in unison. Every tree on one side of the river for a thousand feet was flashing and going dark at exactly the same time.

Something deep inside me warms at the thought that such a patient, careful, and scientific observer, whose curiosity about the world led him so far away from his normal life in the Pacific Northwest, could be rewarded that night by such a magical moment of nature.

Once his capacity for mental reasoning returned, he realized that the trees were not, in fact, glowing; rather, they were covered with a critical number of bioluminescent lightning bugs, all illuminating at the exact same time. Upon returning home, Dr. Smith wrote up a journal article on his discovery of the synchronous lightning bugs. It seemed too good to be true, like something out of a storybook. I'm sadly unsurprised by the next part of the story. He was not believed. Biologists ridiculed his account, even calling it fabricated. Why would male fireflies glow in unison, which would only decrease their chances of distinguishing themselves to potential mates? Mathematicians were equally skeptical. How could order come from chaos in nature without a leader to direct it? And entomologists asked how millions of fireflies could see enough other fireflies to create the exact same pattern, given the limited visibility in the mangrove forest. It seemed physically, mathematically, and biologically impossible.

Yet, it wasn't. And now, thanks to modern science, we know how and why. Turns out that this puzzling behavior actually serves an evolutionary purpose for the fireflies. As published in the prestigious journal *Science,* researchers Moiseff and Cope-land found that when lightning bugs light up at random times, the likelihood of a female responding to a male in the deep, dark recesses of a mangrove forest is 3 percent. But when the lightning bugs light up together, the likelihood of females responding is 82 percent.[2] That's not a typo. **The success rate increased by 79 percentage points when flashing as an interconnected community rather than as individuals.**

Society teaches that it's better to be the only bright light than be in a forest of bright lights. After all, isn't that the way we think about success in our schools and companies? We want to graduate at the top of our class, get the job at the best company, and be chosen to work on the most coveted project. We want our child to be the smartest kid at school, the most popular kid on the block, the fastest kid on the team. When any resource—be it acceptance to the most prestigious university, an interview with a top-ranking company, or a spot on the best athletic team—is limited, we are taught that we have to compete in order to differentiate ourselves from the rest of the pack.

And yet, my research shows that this isn't actually the case. The lightning bug researchers discovered that when the fireflies were able to time their pulses with one another with astonishing accuracy (to the millisecond!), it allowed them to space themselves apart perfectly, thus eliminating the need to compete. In the same way, when we help others become better, we can actually increase the available opportunities, instead of vying for them. Like the lightning bugs, once we learn to co-ordinate and collaborate with those around us, we all begin to shine brighter, both individually and as an ecosystem.

But pause to think for a moment. How did lightning bugs even do it? How did they all coordinate their flashing lights so perfectly, especially given their limited visibility and vision? Researchers Mirollo and Strogatz from Boston College and MIT found in the *Journal of Applied Mathematics* that, amazingly, the fireflies do not have to see everybody to create coordinated action; so long as no group of fireflies is completely out of sight of any other group, they can sync up with one another's rhythms.[3] In other words, it only takes a few nodes to transform the entire system.[4]

Our new understanding of "positive systems" teaches us that the same is true for humans. As you will discover in this book, by becoming a "positive node" in your workplace, company, or community, and helping those around you improve their creativity, their productivity, their abilities, their performance, and more, you are not only helping the group become better; you are exponentially increasing your own potential for success.

There is one final important detail to this intriguing story. Biologists who have explored these jungles now know that the glow emanating from those mangroves can be seen for miles. This means it is even easier for *other* fireflies to find their way to the light. So the brighter it shines, the more newcomers join and add their light. This is true just as much for humans as it is for fireflies: The more you help people find their light, the brighter you both will shine.

THE POWER OF OTHERS

When George Lucas originally wrote the script to the billion-dollar Star Wars franchise, the most iconic line in movie history—"May the Force be with you"—was not in it. Instead, the earliest versions read, "May the Force *of Others* be with you." What does this arcane piece of movie history have to do with the science of potential? As the children's book author Roald Dahl wrote: "The greatest secrets are always hidden in the most unlikely places." And I believe that hidden in this tiny line lies both the problem undergirding our broken pursuit of potential as a society and the secret to exponentially increasing our success, well-being, and happiness.

Our society has become overly focused on the "power of one alone" versus "the power of one made stronger by others." Of course, Hollywood glorifies individual superstars; where else are the streets literally paved with their names? But when we adopt this script in our companies and schools, focusing only on individual achievement and eliminating "others" from the equation, our true power remains hidden. But what is hidden can be revealed.

Three years ago, as I was researching the hidden connections that underlie success and human potential, I had a breakthrough. I became a father.

When my son, Leo, came into the world, he was quite literally helpless. He couldn't even roll over by himself. But, as he got older, he became more capable. And with each new skill he picked up, like any good positive psychology researcher would, I found myself praising him, saying, "Leo, you did that all by yourself! I'm proud of you." And after a while, Leo began parroting it back to me in a soft but proud voice: "All by myself."

That's when I realized: First as children, then as adults in the workplace, we are conditioned to disproportionately value things we accomplish on our own. As a father, if I stopped my praise and guidance there, my son might come to view independent achievement as the ultimate test of our mettle. But in reality it is not. There is a whole other level.

The cycle begins at a young age. At school, our kids are trained to study diligently and individually so they can best others on exams. If they seek help on projects from other students, they are chastised for cheating. They are given multiple hours of homework a night, forcing them to trade time with others for more time working in isolation. Over and over they are reminded that their future success in the workplace hinges on individual metrics, including their grades and standardized test scores. Statistically it doesn't, but this approach to learning does do one thing: It dramatically raises their stress levels while robbing them of social connection, sleep, attention, happiness, and health. Yet, instead of questioning the system, we judge those who can't keep up with this feeding frenzy for individual achievement. By the time students finish school they are frazzled, fragile, and lonely, only to find that the success and happiness they had been promised did not lie at the end of that rainbow.

Suddenly, those same people who tested so well individually struggle when they need to work with others to bring a product to market or get their team to hit a target. Meanwhile, the people who rise to the top are not those who try to do everything all by themselves, but, rather, those who can ask others for help and rally others to grow. Parents who support a balanced, connected approach to pursuing success for their children are rewarded for their persistence, while parents who urge individual achievement at the cost of connection find themselves unprepared for their child's burnout or loneliness.

We spend the first twenty-two years of our life being

judged and praised for our individual attributes and what we can achieve alone, when, for the rest of our life, our success is almost entirely interconnected with that of others.

Over the past decade I have worked with nearly half of the Fortune 100 companies and traveled to more than fifty countries to learn how people everywhere approach the concepts of success, happiness, and human potential. One thing I've found to be true almost everywhere is that the vast majority of companies, schools, and organizations measure and reward "high performance" in terms of individual metrics such as sales numbers, résumé accolades, and test scores. The problem with this approach is that it is predicated on a belief we thought science had fully confirmed: that we live in a world of "survival of the fittest." It teaches us that success is a zero-sum game; that those with the *best* grades, or the *most* impressive résumé, or the *highest* point score, will be the ONLY ones to prosper. The formula is simple: Be better and smarter and more creative than everyone else, and you will be successful.

But this formula is inaccurate.

Thanks to groundbreaking new research you will read about in this book, we now know that achieving our highest potential is not about survival of the fittest; it is **survival of the best fit.** In other words, success is not just about how creative or smart or driven you are, but how well you are able to connect with, contribute to, and benefit from the ecosystem of people around you. It isn't just how highly rated your college or workplace is, but how well you fit in there. It isn't just how many points you score, but how well you complement the skills of the team.

We often think if we can just work harder, faster, and smarter, then we'll achieve our highest potential. But scientifically in the modern world, the biggest impediment to your success and realizing your potential is not lack of productivity, hard work, or intelligence; it is the way in which we pursue it. The pursuit of potential must not be a lonely road. The conclusion of a decade of research is clear: It's not faster alone; it's better together.

By clinging to the old formula for success we are leaving enormous amounts of potential untapped. I saw this firsthand during my twelve years at Harvard as I watched students crash upon shoals of hyper-competition, then get stranded on the banks of self-doubt and stress. Realizing that they were no longer the only superstar, many panicked. They pushed themselves harder, sequestering themselves so they could go faster, trying to be the brightest light shining. The result was darkness. A staggering 80 percent of Harvard students report going through depression at some point in their college life.

Now that I have done this work all over the globe, I know this is not a problem reserved for Ivy League students. The average age of being diagnosed with depression in 1978 was twenty-nine. In 2009, the *average* age was fourteen and a half.[5] Over the past decade, depression rates for adults have doubled, as have hospitalizations for attempted suicide for children as young as eight years old.[6] What could possibly have changed so much to account for this? And, more important, what can we do to fix it?

Our emphasis on individual achievement has gone into serious overdrive, fueled primarily by two significant shifts. First, the rise of technology and social media allows us to broadcast individual accomplishments 24/7, constantly feeding competition while simultaneously stoking insecurity. Second, the astronomical pressure and competition in our schools and companies in pursuit of higher individual success metrics are driving longer days, less sleep, and more stress. Luckily, a better way has begun to emerge.

This exciting new path was inspired by my initial work studying happiness. In *The Happiness Advantage,* I wrote how you can significantly increase your own happiness by doing things such as gratitude exercises, practicing optimism, and meditating. But at some point, if you make these things only about *your* happiness, you reach an invisible limit where happiness can neither be sustained nor grow. The only way to lift that ceiling is to use your own happiness as a fuel to make others happier. Ultimately, I realized that while **happiness is a choice, it is not just an individual choice; it is an interconnected one**. This is because when you choose to act with gratitude or joy, you make joy and gratitude easier for others, who in turn give you more reasons to be grateful and joyous.

Armed with this discovery, I dug into the new research, and it became clear: Happiness was only the tip of the iceberg. Now, thanks to the advent of Big Data, I could finally see the connections that had previously remained hidden. Before, we could only ask questions like "How smart are you?" or "How creative are you?" or "How hard do you work?" But now, we can ask the bigger questions: "How smart do you make others around you?" "How much creativity do you inspire?" "How much does your drive become contagious to a team or family?" "How resilient do you make others?" And when we do, we see that our greatest successes don't exist in isolation. As the research begins to emerge, we seem to be learning that **almost every attribute of your potential—from intelligence to creativity to leadership to personality and engagement—is interconnected with others**. Thus, to truly thrive physically, emotionally, and spiritually, we need to change our pursuit of potential in the same way we need to change our pursuit of happiness: We need to stop trying to be faster alone, and start working to become stronger together.

By creating hyper-competitive environments in which only individual achievements are celebrated, companies and schools are leaving enormous amounts of talent, productivity, and creativity on the table. Overemphasizing the individual and removing others from the equation places a "soft cap" on our potential, an artificial limit on what we can achieve. But the good news is that I call this a *soft* cap for a reason: Because it can be lifted. Because when we work to help others achieve success, we not only raise the performance of the group, we exponentially increase our own potential. This is what I describe later in this book as a Virtuous Cycle—a positive feedback loop whereby making others better leads to more resources, energy, and experiences that make *you* better, fueling the cycle again. Thus, making others better takes *your success* to the next level. Thus:

> SMALL POTENTIAL is the limited success you can achieve alone.
> BIG POTENTIAL is the success you can achieve only in a Virtuous Cycle with others.

In this book, I describe eight original research projects I have conducted with others as well as cutting-edge research from academics that unites neuroscience, psychology, and network analysis to shape the new field of positive systems research. But I know you did not come to this book looking simply for a review of research; there are better books for that. Instead, you want things you can start to implement today. So I have spent the past three years crafting a practical approach to Big Potential based on this science and my work at NASA, the NFL, the White House, and elsewhere, as well as my conversations with highly successful people, including Will Smith, Oprah Winfrey, and Michael Strahan, who are living the principles of Big Potential.

This path consists of five stages, what I call the SEEDS of Big Potential: SURROUND yourself with a Star System of Positive Influencers. EXPAND your power by helping others lead from every seat. ENHANCE your resources by becoming a Prism of Praise. DEFEND the system against negative attacks. And SUSTAIN the gains by fueling the Virtuous Cycle. Seeds are the perfect metaphor for this research, because a seed cannot grow alone, without the help of the sun, soil, and water. In the same way, you can grow your potential, but you can't grow it alone. The biggest growth is achieved when you tap into the potential of those around you.

We can no longer be content competing for the scraps of Small Potential; we must seek new frontiers of human potential and invite others to follow. A challenging world demands that we put "the force *of others*" back into our formula. And it all starts by finding the hidden connections between flashing bugs, nudity at Harvard, featherless chickens, and an awkward dance with Oprah.

brain fog I wondered if this was actually happening, or if the pressures of Harvard had cracked my brain. Then they began to scream.

A moment ago we talked about the lightning bugs of the mangrove forests who lure their mates by synchronously flashing their luminous light into the dark night sky. Well, I was about to experience a collective "flashing" of a rather different kind.

Every year, on the midnight before exams begin, Harvard students take part in what's called the Primal Scream, a venerable tradition that some attribute to our clearly not-so-puritanical forebears. While Founding Father John Adams was making his mark upon history by signing the Declaration of Independence, his son Charles was earning a mark of distinction for being caught streaking with his friends in Harvard Yard.[1] They were thrown out of the school, then later readmitted (clearly if your father is a Founding Father you get at least one get-out-of-jail-free card), and their chilly tradition continues today. More than three hundred years later, the bravest and/or most intoxicated students gather in front of Mower Hall, where they proceed to disrobe. Then the half-frozen, fully naked students begin to jog in a tight pack over the icy ground of old Harvard Yard, huddling together for warmth as hundreds of onlookers come streaming out of their dorms. And for a few brief moments, the anxiety of failing to reach one's potential on exams is replaced by the (very real) fears of potential frostbite—not to mention potential embarrassment in front of one's peers.

This was my first exposure—if you will excuse the pun—to Primal Scream. Now, let me pause for those of you who don't know me to give you two salient facts. First, prior to arriving at Harvard, I had lived most of my life in Waco, Texas, where not only was wearing clothes heavily encouraged, but where streaking in the snow would have been unheard of—because there is no snow. Second, I'm shy. I'd never been to a club, never approached a girl in a bar, and never gone skinny-dipping. And yet, as I watched the spectacle that night from my first-floor dorm window, I worried that I was truly missing out on college. Here I was, cloistered in a dorm, reading about life in Rome under Augustus, while my peers were actually living their lives to the fullest. So I decided to join.

My fatigue-addled brain decided the best strategy would be to undress in my room, then simply wait for the rest of the group to pass by on their way to the Yard, and then just stealthily slip into their ranks under the cover of the dark. As the door banged shut behind me, I immediately realized my first mistake. Being from Texas, it hadn't occurred to me that shoes are pretty crucial for a run—naked or otherwise—in the snow. Then I realized my second mistake: I had left my ID card, needed to re-enter the building, in the pocket of my pants, which I of course had left crumpled up on the floor of my dorm room. That's when I realized my third, and perhaps biggest, mistake. I was alone. There was no way I was going to be able to slip into the crowd without drawing attention to myself. After all, if you are flashing people in a group, yours is just one face in the crowd. If you try to streak solo like Will Ferrell in *Old School,* everyone knows it is you.

As I stood there in the dead of winter, thinking about which extremity I would least like to lose, an equally shy, library-bound dorm mate walked out with an armful of books. She squeaked, then we both resorted to an age-old strategy: If we pretend not to see something, we can convince ourselves it never happened. Red-faced and blue-toed, I snuck in the door, entered my room, and re-robed as fast as humanly possible. For the remainder of the four years I was there, she never mentioned my aborted attempt at a three-hundred-year-old tradition: My naked run ended two feet from my door. And I certainly didn't mention that she was the only girl to see me naked during my undergrad years at Harvard.

Now, this book is rated PG-13 for nudity, scientific language, and occasional adult situations. But I tell this story not because of its prurient details, but because it so powerfully demonstrates a cold, hard truth: There are certain things in this world that require the support of other people and that should never be attempted alone. Pursuing potential alone is a bit like being that shoeless freshman who never actually made it to the naked run at the Yard; it's cold, it's lonely, and you're not likely to get very far. Running in a pack, however, is more like what happens when you tap into the power of Big Potential; you can make it much farther—even in extreme conditions—than you can on your own.

Reid Hoffman, the cofounder and chairman of LinkedIn, sums it up well: "No matter how brilliant your mind or strategy, if you're playing a solo game, you'll always lose out to a team." Steve Jobs, the late founder and CEO of one of the most competitive and powerful companies ever built, said, "Great things in business are never done by one person. They're done by a team of people." Navy SEALs during training sometimes link arms when they do push-ups to promote going through stress "together," rather than in isolation. And the SEALs have a great saying: "Individuals play the game, but teams beat the odds."

The Primal Scream ritual at Harvard is evidence that in times of stress, we need others to link arms with more than ever. This conclusion was borne out by a study published in *Nature* that found that, based on analysis of eighty thousand interactions among college students, the highest achievers were those who formed the most social connections and shared information in more ways.[2] And in incredible research published in the *Journal of Experimental Social Psychology*, the researchers found that if you are looking at a hill and judging how steep it is, the mere presence of social support around you transforms your perception. In fact, if you look at a hill while standing next to someone you consider to be a friend, the hill looks 10 to 20 percent less steep than if you were facing that hill alone.[3] That is a *stunning* finding. **Perception of your objective, physical world is transformed by including others in your pursuit of achievement.** This result holds even if the friend is three feet away, facing the other direction, and silent! This makes evolutionary sense. Other people provide resources and support. So, mentally and physically, mountains seem more climbable, successes more achievable, and obstacles more surmountable with others beside us.

So why do people in the midst of stress at work retreat into their offices, sequestering themselves from colleagues in order to get their work done? Why do college students respond to pressure and stress by withdrawing from friends, fleeing to a secluded corner of the library, or consuming copious amounts of caffeine, Adderall, and antidepressants? When I read the admission files of hundreds of students as a freshman proctor at Harvard, the number of students requesting a single dorm room as opposed to one with roommates was staggering. This wasn't because the single rooms were bigger or nicer; it was because they mistakenly believed that the presence of people around them would distract them or blunt their competitive edge. But in doing so, these students were missing out on the one thing that really predicts long-term success and well-being: others. Which is why Harvard so desperately needed a class called Psych 1504.

A CRUCIAL DISCOVERY

Dr. Tal Ben-Shahar was way ahead of the curve. He began to teach positive psychology at Harvard before anyone had even heard it was a subject. Not long after my failed flashing experiment, an experimental seminar was being taught by one of the most thoughtful and authentic professors at Harvard. The following year, Tal invited me to join him as the head teaching fellow for Psych 1504, which would open up positive psychology to the whole university. On day one, the crowds were a fire hazard even though Harvard had given us the biggest room on campus. Over the next two years, one out of every five Harvard students ended up taking the course; it seemed that Harvard students were particularly eager to learn about how to improve emotional well-being in a hyper-competitive environment.

During that time, I designed and ran one of the largest studies of human potential that have been done at Harvard. Sixteen hundred Harvard students filled out a battery of validated psychometric tools and other questions that took almost an hour to complete. My goal was to determine the matrix of individual attributes that would predict who would be happiest and most successful at Harvard. In other words, could I predict the perfect Harvard student? The data set was so big that my puny, inexpensive laptop kept crashing. I had information on everything from students' family income, their high school GPA and SAT scores, and the number of hours they slept to how many classes they were taking, how many clubs they were involved in, and more.

But as I started doing my analysis, I soon noticed a problem. The individual attributes of these students had almost no correlation with their performance and success! Statistically, the students who had perfect SAT scores could also be getting all C's. Students with almost no money were equally happy and had the same grades as their rich peers. The number of friends on Facebook was predictive of nothing, not even extraversion. Just as I was becoming increasingly frustrated at having gone to all the work only to find virtually no significant correlations, I finally stumbled on a massive exception: social connection.

Using the most famously validated scale that measures how interconnected and socially supported an individual feels in their life, I found that social connection was, hands down, the greatest predictor of thriving both personally and academically at Harvard. It was the strongest predictor of emotional well-being and optimism, the greatest buffer against depression, and it also predicted how much stress one felt in the face of exams and academic competition. And it turns out, once someone leaves college, it becomes one of the greatest predictors of long-term performance in their careers. The evidence seemed to suggest a wild conclusion: Success at Harvard was less about the individual attributes of a student and more about how they fit in with the culture and with their peers. Or, put another way, **the potential to succeed at Harvard had less to do with "survival of the fittest" and more to do with "survival of the best fit."**

While it would seem that those who would succeed were the superstars who could shine the brightest, in reality, the flashes of brilliance were actually coming from those who had found their place within a constellation of stars. And, as I would soon learn, this concept is equally true well beyond the walls of Harvard, with powerful implications for how we think about potential within our companies, our teams, and in our lives and careers.

REWORKING OUR DEFINITION OF POTENTIAL

A year before writing this book, I was invited to speak at a conference at Google called re:Work. This conference was designed to "open source" good ideas for organizational change. The night before my talk, I attended a dinner at a dimly lit, cedarwood-paneled vegan restaurant (which was exactly what I expected from California and from Google), where I was seated next to a smiling man whom I didn't recognize, but who asked some very interesting questions about my research. It wasn't until the next morning, when that man got onstage, that I learned he was not only the leader of the conference but also one of the most respected business leaders in the world.

Laszlo Bock was the head of the world-renowned People Operations department at Google. He possesses a mix of kind leadership and focused brilliance that has surely contributed to his success in making Google the number-one company to work for year after year, and earned him the distinction of "HR Professional of the Decade." As he describes in his bestselling book *Work Rules!*, the lynchpin of the company's uncanny ability to consistently hire the most creative and high-potential employees lies, perhaps not surprisingly, in Google's practice of collecting enormous amounts of data about pretty much everything.

"Big Data" is the term used for the massive digital data sets generated each time we visit a website, use social media, make an online purchase, and so on. This concept has gotten a lot of attention over recent years, as the sophisticated algorithms we can now use to mine that data for trends and patterns have allowed us to reach powerful insights into human behavior. Big Data is changing everything, from how companies do business and how governments understand population trends to how doctors and public health workers detect disease. But what is less known is that Big Data is also one of the best tools we have at our disposal to help us understand Big Potential. Now that we have so much data at our fingertips, we aren't limited to merely measuring individual attributes such as intelligence, creativity, or happiness. We can now evaluate our impact upon *others'* intelligence, creativity, and happiness.

So a few months later, when Oprah's team asked me to find her five leaders to interview for our course on happiness, I jumped at the chance to call Laszlo in the hopes of learning how one of the most successful companies in the world predicts greatness and potential. In other words, I wanted to know about Project Aristotle.

To crack the code on true potential, the data scientists on Google's world-famous People Analytics team launched a Big Data initiative with the not-so-secret code name Project Aristotle. Here was their initial mission: Build the perfect team. On the surface, that task might seem straightforward. If you are going to build a dream team, simply fill it with the highest performing individuals, right? So the next question is, what specific qualities would you look for? High IQ? Fluency in several languages? The ability to quickly solve quadratic equations in one's head? Essentially that is what Project Aristotle was utilizing the greatest algorithm technology in history to find out. By analyzing incredible amounts of data—including tens of thousands of responses across 180 teams—on everything from introversion to skill set to intelligence to personality to backgrounds, Project Aristotle sought to create the profile that would make for the perfect performer in the workplace. The conclusion was astonishing and challenged everything you might think you know about potential.

They found there *is* no profile of a "perfect performer." Project Aristotle reached more or less the same conclusion as my study at Harvard: When it comes to potential, individual traits and aptitudes are poor predictors of success on a team. One of the leaders in Google's prestigious People Analytics division, Abeer Dubey, put it succinctly: "At Google, we're good at finding patterns. There weren't strong patterns here. *The 'who' part of the equation didn't seem to matter.*"[4] Wow! Take that in for a moment. The company that has become the best at searching for patterns in all of human history could not find a pattern in which individual skills, honed in isolation, predicted the success of an individual in a team. In other words, it isn't how smart you are, how many degrees you have, what your personality is like, or what grades you received; it isn't how many AP courses you took, how creative you are, or how many languages you can read. It is, to take us back to the beginning, "survival of the best fit." As I had found at Harvard, and as Google confirmed using the best data technology available, those are the wrong variables to be measuring when trying to calculate success and potential. Why? Because they were *individual* attributes. The "who" of the equation, in other words, measures only your Small Potential. And Small Potential doesn't come anywhere close to predicting your full capacity for success at work and in life.

And yet, that "who" is what we mistakenly focus on in admission files, on job applications, in interviews, and in other forms of evaluation. Similar to how Dr. Smith's discovery about the synchronous fireflies led scientists to question everything they believed they knew about animal behavior, Google seemed to be questioning something equally fundamental about the nature of potential. How could skill sets and intelligence and personality and background *not* have a statistical advantage in predicting achievement?

And if those individual attributes don't predict success and potential, what does? The answer is clear: It is all about the ecosystem around you. Project Aristotle found that if the individuals on the team had (1) high "social sensitivity"—that is, a strong awareness of the importance of social connections—and (2) if the team had cultivated an environment where each person spoke just about equally and everyone felt safe sharing their ideas, the team hit their highest levels of performance over and over and over. In other words, success at Google, just like at Harvard, isn't about survival of the fittest; it is about survival of the best fit.

For decades, we have been measuring intelligence at the individual level, just as we have been measuring creativity, engagement, and grit. But it turns out we were failing to measure something with far greater impact. As reported in the journal *Science*, researchers from MIT, Union College, and Carnegie Mellon have finally found a method for systematically measuring the intelligence of a *group* as opposed to an individual.[5] Just as we evaluate how successful an individual student will be at solving a problem, we are now able to predict how successful a *group* of people will be at solving a problem or problems. Again, it would be easy to assume that if you put a group of high-IQ people together, naturally they would exhibit a high collective intelligence. But that's not what happens. Indeed, their research found that a team on which each person was merely average in their individual abilities but possessed a *collective* intelligence would continually exhibit higher success rates than a team of individual geniuses.

The researchers concluded that the "general collective intelligence factor that explains the group's performance on a wide variety of tasks" was "a *property of the group itself, not just the individuals in it.*" In other words, the smartest group isn't necessarily the one with the smartest people in it. Or, as Aristotle once famously said, "The whole is greater than the sum of its parts."

This represents a completely different way for us to look at performance at work. I have given more than eight hundred talks for "high-potential" employees, yet thanks to new research I will share in this book, I now know that what they are really measuring is Small Potential. My research team and I were starting to discover something startling: Your potential is way bigger than you. Your success, your well-being, and your performance are all connected to that of the people around you. Incredibly, we found that the traits contributing to your success are linked in such a way that when you help those around you become better, you raise not only the collective performance of the group but that of everyone in it. Because, as you'll see in the pages and chapters ahead, when you work to help make others more successful, **you in turn take the invisible cap off your own success.**

THE ECOSYSTEM OF POTENTIAL

When the gray wolf was reintroduced into Yellowstone National Park, there was only one beaver colony left in the entire park, due in part to overgrazing by the large population of elk. But the reintroduction of wolves into the environment kept the elk moving so they didn't stay nibbling the willows, which allowed the trees to grow, providing the lumber the beavers needed for their dams. The beavers returned, the vegetation flourished; balance was restored. Incredibly, that one improvement led to a cascade of ripple effects that transformed the entire ecosystem.

We can see similar ripple effects across what I call the Ecosystem of Potential: the network of connections that determines our success and our outcomes. For many years, companies, schools, and communities all over the world have been measuring success and potential in a limited way. They all assumed that traits that contribute to our potential, from intelligence to engagement to creativity and even to health, were individual and fixed, end of the story. Then they would make huge assumptions—about everything from which candidate to hire or promote (and what to pay them) to what company to invest in and which student to admit—based on a single data point, like your individual sales target, or where you went to graduate school, or your IQ score. They simply had no way to measure anything beyond how well one person did on a test, or meeting a sales goal, alone.

But now we know that the traits that contribute to our potential are neither individual nor fixed; rather, they are linked across our ecosystem. And with the help of Big Data and positive systems research, we now have the requisite tools and rich data sets that allow us to see patterns that were previously hidden. Specifically, for the first time in history, we have begun to quantify the impact that each of us has on those around us, and in turn the influence others have on us, as well.

At the heart of the initial research on the Ecosystem of Potential is . . . well, a heart. Actually, five thousand hearts. The famous Framingham Heart Study, which began in 1948, is now one of the most important studies validating the ideas underlying Big Potential. Nearly seventy years later, in 2017, I was invited to speak at the National Institutes of Health, the group responsible for funding this deep-dive look into the risk factors of heart disease. The decades-long study in Framingham, Massachusetts, has revealed powerful findings about the relationship between social connections and our cardiovascular health. While the results of their research are far too wide-reaching and complex to fully address here, the main takeaway I had from that meeting was that they found having healthy individuals in our community or network actually increases the chances that we ourselves will be healthier. These findings, and others like them, have kicked the door wide open for an entire field of study that combines positive psychology with Big Data to show how powerfully our social ecosystem impacts so much more than just our physical health.

Meanwhile, across the Charles River, researcher Nicholas Christakis from Harvard Medical School linked up with James Fowler from UC San Diego to take this line of research one step further. If our physical health is interconnected, they wondered, might our emotional health and happiness be interconnected as well?[6] Incredibly, Fowler and Christakis found that it was more interconnected than we ever imagined. According to their analysis, **if you became happier, any friend within a one-mile radius would be 63 percent more likely to also become happier.** Wow! And by the same token, they found that if you are currently not happy but surround yourself with happy people, your likelihood of finding happiness increases dramatically. In short, being surrounded by happy people doesn't guarantee you happiness, but it significantly improves your chances.

But this is just the tip of the iceberg. Now we know that our health and our happiness aren't the only traits that are interconnected. Personality, creativity, energy, engagement, leadership, and even sales performance are all predicted by those you surround yourself with. **In other words, connecting with high-potential people dramatically increases your likelihood of high-potential outcomes.**

In a landmark study published in one of the most prestigious psychology journals (the *Journal of Personality and Social Psychology*), researchers from Michigan State blew open our understanding of personality not as a constellation of individual traits but as a set of interconnected ones. It turns out that not only do the people around us powerfully shape the type of person we'll become, but that their influence begins to take root at a very young age. For example, they found that when three- or four-year-old children were surrounded by peers who were hardworking or social, they too would begin to work harder and be more social.[*]

Similarly, they found that if children were surrounded by people who are attentive, careful, and playful, they would adopt those traits into themselves. And on the flip side, when children were surrounded by people who couldn't sustain attention and were disobedient or impulsive, the kids too became disobedient or impulsive.[7] Jennifer Watling Neal, one of the authors of the study, wrote, **"Our finding, that personality traits are contagious among children, flies in the face of common assumptions that personality is ingrained and can't be changed."**

Other traits, including patience, energy, and introversion/extraversion, are also "contagious." When researchers in Paris asked participants to make a series of decisions after observing the decisions of undercover researchers (who were actually artificial intelligence algorithms), it turned out that when the

---

[*] This was a longitudinal study, so they could see how effort control, positive and negative emotions, and social play changed over time.

participants observed lazier decisions, they were more likely to make lazy decisions; when they observed patient and prudent decisions, they were more patient and prudent in their own decision-making.[8] And while it is all too easy to label oneself as high energy or low energy, an introvert or an extravert, researchers find that traits like these are "situationally dependent" on the people you surround yourself with. According to Professor Brian Little at Harvard, a mild introvert becomes more extraverted in a group of more introverted people, while the mild extravert becomes quiet and more introverted in the presence of loud, more extraverted extraverts.

Even genius is interconnected. If I asked you to name some of the most iconic geniuses throughout history, who would come to mind? Einstein, Edison, and Shakespeare? Our culture portrays individuals like these as towering, larger-than-life figures who could go into a room alone and come out with earth-shattering ideas. But this is not the reality. Edison, for example, was one of the most prolific inventors of our time, with more than 1,900 patents. Yet, historians struggle to determine if he ever invented anything himself. In truth, most of the inventions credited to Edison were actually created in collaboration with the team of inventors who worked with him.[9] That is not to say he was not brilliant, but rather that he is a perfect example of what we can achieve when we recognize that potential is interconnected. Edison was able to become one of the most important inventors of all time because by helping his team become more creative, he tapped into the full power of his ecosystem. That's Big Potential.

My former Shakespeare professor Marjorie Garber once gave a lecture saying that the meaning of the word "genius" has been distorted over the ages. Originally, she says, you could "have genius" but you couldn't BE a genius. No one could "own" inspiration because, by definition, to be inspired means that you were the recipient. My friend and one of my favorite people in this world is Liz Gilbert, the famous author of *Eat Pray Love*. In her book *Big Magic*, she argues that we must return to the idea that all great geniuses have Muses who inspire and coax greatness out of them. One of my favorite parts of her book is where she describes a writer who would literally dress up and strut around the room to convince Inspiration that he is worthy of its attention. My point is that **Big Potential, like genius, creativity, and inspiration, is not something you HAVE; it is something you tap into.**

Contrary to the myth of the lone genius, innovation and creativity have so much less to do with individual attributes or aptitudes and so much more to do with those around you. Why do you think that some of the modern world's greatest artistic achievements have emerged out of the gathering of composers, writers, and artists in salons, artists' collectives, or colonies? Why do you think musicians and "cultural creatives" go to festivals, and writers congregate at secluded writers' retreats? It's because they know that being around other creative people is the best way to get the creative energies flowing. This is what I call in chapter 3 "positive peer pressure."

In the workplace, too, we need other people to inspire us and coax out our creativity. In one study, researchers found that employees who work in an environment with a transformative leader—one who inspires with a clear vision and encourages subordinates to create new ideas and outlooks—were significantly more creative and mentally flexible (a condition for innovation) than those who work for a transactional leader—one who offers praise and rewards in direct exchange for high performance done in isolation.[10]

The ecosystem around us can even have a profound impact on how moral and charitable we are. In one of my all-time favorite studies, researcher Katie Carman went into a company of seventy-five employees and found out exactly how much each one normally donated to the United Way. Then she looked at what happened when an employee was moved to another part of the company—that is, had new influences. Incredibly, she found that when someone who didn't normally give was moved to sit near people who did, every dollar increase in the average donations by the nearby coworkers resulted in an increase of $.53 for the moved employee.[11] Our willingness to be generous is not just an individual choice. We are constantly shaping and being shaped by how others give, forgive, and invest in one another.

Even the process of learning itself is impacted by those around us. Researchers at Stanford and Vanderbilt proved this powerfully with a program they designed called Betty's Brain. Betty is an online animated character they brought into middle school classrooms to see what would happen when students were instructed to teach "her" the principles of environmental science.[12] The result was that the students spent significantly more time going over and over the material, and developed a higher level of understanding and mastery of it. We learn better when we teach others rather than study simply for the sake of individual knowledge. This is called the "protégé effect."[13] And it's a perfect example of how working to make others better actually increases your individual potential.

These connections are what allow us to magnify what is possible as a mere individual. It is one thing to be smart enough to learn a language. It is much more impressive to be able to help others learn to speak it. It is one thing to learn resilience and survival skills. It is much more impressive to be able to help wounded victims survive a storm. It is one thing to be self-motivated at work. It is much more impressive to motivate a team to be successful in the midst of uncertainty. *There is only so much you can achieve if you strive only to improve yourself; it is time we began to pursue success and achievement in a markedly different way.*

We are taught that to achieve our potential, we must best each other in cutthroat competition, first at school and then in the workplace. But once we understand how success is interconnected, suddenly another, better path begins to emerge. *Big Potential isn't about trying to go faster alone. It's about working to become better together.*

FEATHERLESS AND PECKED TO DEATH

As a young researcher, William Muir had staked his entire academic future on a hunch about bugs, fish, and barnyard animals. Ever since Darwin published his famous theory of natural selection, the idea of survival of the fittest has been central to our understanding of biology and genetics. Muir, however, believed that when it comes to evolutionary success, it's not individual natural selection but rather *group selection* that matters. Unfortunately, science had already discounted group selection as being ridiculous, and Muir was advised that if he wanted to rise in the ranks of academia, he would do well to abandon this pursuit.

While these might seem like arcane academic disputes, the distinction between these two theories goes to the heart of nearly everything we believe about human potential. It also shows why science is slow to learn.

Determined to open the eyes of the scientific community to the merits of this theory, Muir did a brilliant study—later made even more famous by a TED Talk by Margaret Heffernan—that revealed a surprising truth with far-reaching implications.[14] Imagine you're a CEO of a chicken farm (bear with me here) and you want to breed the highest-producing group of chickens. What's the best strategy? Previous theories on genes and evolution give an easy answer: Find the chickens who produce the most eggs, take them and breed them with other high producers to create a new generation of even higher-performing chickens, then rinse and repeat until you have the most elite chicken farm in the world. So that's what Muir did, for seven generations of chickens. At the same time, he kept a second "normal" group—a mix of both high- and low-producing chickens—and bred them for seven generations. According to the theory of natural selection, one would expect that by the last generation the first group would yield a flock of superstar chickens. Yet, it didn't. In fact, Muir was actually forced to stop the experiment early, because all but three of the hyper-productive chickens had been pecked to death (and those three hens did not emerge unscathed, having had all of their feathers plucked off).[15] The chickens in the normal group, on the other hand, not only survived, they were all still covered with feathers. In fact, they produced 160 percent more eggs than did the "MVP" chickens.

Muir's gamble had paid off. "You can waste energy by maintaining a pecking order," he explained. "But if animals don't care about a pecking order and they get along, *that energy is transferred to production.*" In other words, when members of a group—be they human beings or chickens—focus only on competing their way to the top, they are likely to peck one another to death. When they work to lift one another up, however, everybody wins.

This conclusion has important implications for how we think about performance in both schools and in organizations. "If a pig or chicken rises to the top of the ladder by stepping on the shoulders, or heads, of others, then a breeding program doesn't make progress,"[16] Muir wrote. I don't know about you, but in the world of business I have personally encountered a lot of pigs who step on others and a lot of chickens who are constantly pecking at anyone around them who tries to be successful. And if you let them continue unchecked, you're left with a few featherless chickens who may have survived but never thrived.

Anytime we try to push against a deeply ingrained mistaken formula for living, we are going to have to expect pushbacks. The first mental barrier to Big Potential is an ego-based one. I remember once speaking to a Wall Street trader who reveled in competition. Within one minute of meeting him, he had already told me how superior his sons were on the soccer and lacrosse fields. When I mentioned the concept of Big Potential, he asked me why in the world I would "want to help someone else be more competitive. Isn't it better to be the smartest or strongest person in the room?"

At first blush, this critique seems to make a lot of sense. And I hear it everywhere. The problem with this view is that it's not capturing the bigger picture. What that strong or smart person can accomplish alone is dwarfed by what they could accomplish when they connect with and improve the performance of the people on their team. When others around you are creative and smart, then you become MORE creative or smart than you were before. Moreover, because our potential is not fixed but, rather, a renewable resource with the power to multiply when we tap into the potential of the people around us, the more we invest in the skills and abilities of others, the more dividends we reap in our own. **You CAN be a superstar; you just can't be a superstar alone.**

This is why the survival-of-the-fittest approach is misguided, and it's also why pursuing Small Potential is both costly and shortsighted. Recall my Harvard potential study and Google's Project Aristotle, which concluded that the "who" part of the equation did not predict long-term success. Muir's research, too, confirms these findings. "Cumulatively those social effects were much more important than that of the individual,"[17] he explains. To achieve these effects, we need to focus not on "breeding" high-performing individuals who will compete with one another to death, but on helping to make the group collectively better.

In our modern workplace, this is truer than ever. As companies and systems are becoming increasingly complex, the achievements of individuals are becoming far less distinguishable—and thus far less important—than the overall results of a team. From legal teams to teams of software programmers and sales teams, employees are being evaluated individually less and less. Moreover, leaders are being evaluated less for their individual performance and more for their ability to activate the higher potential on their team. In sports, some believe that it's the one to score the most points who gets the best draft pick or the biggest scholarship. But scouts don't come to watch losing teams. In the workplace just as on the playing field, it's **better to be a good player on a great team, rather than the star player on a forgettable team**.

And this will only become truer in the years and decades ahead. As researchers at the University of Virginia found, the time spent by employees in collaborative activities has ballooned by 50 percent or more in just two decades. And the aforementioned Google study revealed that today, more than *75 percent* of an employee's day is spent communicating with their coworkers and colleagues.[18] It's fair to say that our potential now is more inextricably linked to others than perhaps at any point in history.

In a world that is changing fast, Big Potential helps us stay resilient. Setbacks are inevitable, both in our lives and in our careers. If you stumble or burn out on your own, it can take a long time to bounce back or recover. But if your success is connected to that of others, you will have a support system to carry you until your energy returns. If you are a lone hyperproductive ant and you get injured, then you're in trouble. But if you are just one of lots of productive ants, then the colony can continue to thrive until you heal. The head of the Center for Complex Network Research, Albert-László Barabási, argues in his book *Linked* that problems in any system are defended against and balanced out by the interconnections. The more we work to make those around us stronger, the more likely it is that we ourselves will be cushioned and supported.

Let me state this very clearly: This book is not an argument against competition in business. **I do not believe competition is bad.** In fact, competition, when set up properly, can dramatically hone our potential, as well as provide joy and energy. As the Dalai Lama says, competition can be productive when "it is used in a good way. It is positive to want to go first, provided the intention is to pave the way for others, make their path easier, help them, or show the way. Competition *is* negative when we wish to defeat others, to bring them down in order to lift ourselves up." **Big Potential is about gaining a competitive advantage not by limiting others' success rates, but by raising them.**

We are often told that there is no innovation without competition, which is absurd given that most of the greatest innovations in science and technology have resulted from the sharing of research across academic silos, national borders, and language barriers. In truth, no great innovations occur in isolation. Personally, I have been asked to sign an obnoxious number of nondisclosure agreements from other researchers terrified that their ideas will get out. But in truth, I've found this approach counterproductive. Those who hold their cards too close to the vest are rarely the ones who play the winning hand. It is when we share our findings with people with other areas of expertise or perspectives, or seek feedback about our concept from someone in a different field, or try out our idea with potential users, that suddenly the real potential starts to emerge.

As W. Edwards Deming, one of the grandfathers of modern organizational development, wrote in a review of Peter Senge's management classic, *The Fifth Discipline,* "People are born with intrinsic motivation, self-respect, dignity, curiosity to learn, joy in learning. The forces of destruction begin with toddlers—a prize for the best Halloween costume, grades in school, gold stars—and on up through the university. On the job, people, teams, and divisions are ranked, reward for the top, punishment for the bottom."[19] If we continue to teach our children—our future employees, our future leaders, and our future innovators—to peck their way to the top, we will constrain their potential as well as that of our businesses and our economy as a whole.

THE VIRTUOUS CYCLE

In my first book, *The Happiness Advantage,* I argued that while people tend to believe that pursuing success will lead to happiness, in fact, the research showed that this relationship was backward; that when we pursue happiness, we are actually more likely to become more successful. Then, too, I received pushback. After all, it's tempting to treat happiness as "nice to have"—to think, "Okay, let me just get through all this work, or let me just land that right job or that promotion; then I can start thinking about this happiness stuff." But over two decades of research proves that this is the wrong path, and one that dramatically limits both your success rates and your happiness.

I am making a similar argument here. It is equally tempting to treat Big Potential as an afterthought—to think, "Okay, once I'm really successful, once I've become a superstar, then I can start thinking about shining that light on others." But the research is stunningly clear that this view, too, is directionally wrong.

In fact, Big Potential doesn't operate in a single direction at all. Instead, it works as a positive feedback loop, whereby successes in our ecosystem create a cascade of compounding successes, or what I call a Virtuous Cycle.

We've all heard the term "vicious cycle" used to describe what happens when cascading negative events become compounded. An employee doesn't like her current job, so she becomes disengaged, which makes her do poorly at work, which makes her dislike her job more. A great home-run hitter strikes out three times in a game, starts to lose confidence, and becomes timid with his swing, which leads to more strikeouts next game, and so forth. But there is a lesser-known alternative to the vicious cycle pattern. **A *Virtuous* Cycle is an upward spiral of potential whereby with each success, you garner more resources, which, in turn, allow you to achieve greater and greater successes.**

Just as a vicious cycle compounds the negative, a Virtuous

Cycle compounds the positive, making future progress easier and easier. For example, a sales leader shares the praise for her sales success with one of her support team members, which makes that member feel more invested—which leads to greater sales success for the leader and in turn to more success and praise. An overworked manager trusts his assistant enough to delegate an important task; this makes that assistant feel trusted, which leads to his knocking it out of the park on the project, thereby earning even more trust from the overworked manager. A student tries to overcome her shyness to talk to someone new at school and ends up making a friend, thereby giving her more confidence in the future to overcome her now-diminishing shyness.

General Colin Powell once said, "Perpetual optimism is a force multiplier." A force multiplier is any object or person in your environment that exponentially increases your power to accomplish far greater things than you could alone. The five strategies in this book have been proven to be true force multipliers. Based on my research and observations working across the globe with places such as NASA, the U.S. Treasury, and the NFL, you'll learn how to plant these seeds into the most fertile ground—that is, to help create environments where you can get the highest yield on your investment in others. No matter your position, age, or title, you can find powerful ways to create Virtuous Cycles of potential by planting these SEEDS in your life.

In the first strategy, SURROUND, I will describe how you can become a superstar by creating a system of stars around you. When you help others shine, the system turns up the light, thereby making your own star brighter.

In the second strategy, I describe how to EXPAND your power to create positive change within your ecosystem by helping others lead from every seat. The more you empower others to spread their own power, the more your impact multiplies.

In the third strategy, I will explain the research on how to EN-HANCE others' potential, which, in turn, creates a higher return on our own. I will show you how to become what I call a "Prism of Praise" and how refracting the light of praise outward not only illuminates others but also enhances our own position.

In DEFEND, I will show you how to protect your Ecosystem of Potential against negative influences to make the entire system more resilient. By being able to handle tougher challenges, you become stronger and thus able to handle larger challenges.

In the final strategy I will show you how to SUSTAIN the gains to your potential, creating collective momentum that lifts your ceiling of potential higher and higher. Successes in isolation are capped, but interconnected successes accelerate and build upon one another.

Together, these SEEDS themselves create a Virtuous Cycle, lifting the ceiling on your potential higher and higher.

I have now worked with countless corporate leaders, spoken to teachers and parents at schools victimized by shootings, learned about the power of positivity from patients just diagnosed with multiple sclerosis, and met with celebrities, all trying to understand the path to Big Potential. Everywhere, I kept hearing the same limiting beliefs repeated over and over: "You cannot change other people." "People are just their genes and environment." "Some people are born that way." We have heard statements like these so many times from teachers, managers, therapists, parents, and coaches that as a society we have begun to accept them. But there is no scientific backing for this. In fact, every study done over the past eight decades in which researchers introduced variables into people's lives that yield significant results is proof you *can* change others. In fact, we change people ALL THE TIME.

I find it so odd when people nod vigorously at the idea that you cannot change other people—and yet five minutes later talk about the toxic effect of negative people in their lives or workplaces. If your day can be ruined by an angry email from a client, a rude encounter with a neighbor, or a bad interaction with your manager, why is the opposite not equally true? Why can't the interactions with the positive people in your life make your day better and the choice to flourish easier?

We ALL have the power to make others better. And when we commit to using that power, there is no limit to what we can accomplish. I believe this not just because of the decades of research, but because I have been experiencing it firsthand in my own life watching my father.

THE BIGGER MEANING

Earlier this year, after thirty-eight years as a neuroscience professor, my father retired. Despite the fact that some of his early research helped jump-start the entire field of neuroscience, he did not fully devote his time to academic publication to build himself up. Instead, my father accepted five times the number of advisees compared to other professors. And he was there to be a dad for my sister and me.

And yet, for much of his career, my father felt like a failure. He wasn't publishing as much as his colleagues who had abandoned their students for more accolades. And he had wanted to follow in the footsteps of his father, a war hero surgeon who won a Navy Cross for performing a tracheotomy under fire after being shot three times. Those are difficult boots to fill, and due to a tumultuous first year at UCLA, my father did not have the grades needed to get into medical school, despite three subsequent years of straight A's. Yet having watched him help hundreds of his own students get into medical school, and having seen him sit with those crying students who didn't get in, helping them see how they might have a different and perhaps better path, I know the truth: He *found his Big Potential* by helping those kids realize theirs.

If you have grown up or resided with someone who felt they hadn't lived up to their potential, you know the heartbreak and sense of powerlessness that come with wanting to help them see their lives more clearly. It is so easy to look at one data point or a single grade or number and miss the truth about someone's successful contribution to the world.

At my father's retirement party, I was asked to give a speech about him to a room packed with people whose lives he had transformed. One minute in, my young son Leo ran up to the stage and lifted his arms and said in his evolutionarily designed piteous voice, "Daddy hold, Daddy hold!" There I was, a proud son celebrating his father, and also a proud father comforting his son . . . and suddenly the concept of *Big Potential* started to make sense in a whole new way.

I thought I already wanted everything for Leo. I wanted him to be happy. I wanted him to be smart. Not just smart, I wanted the first book he read to be *War in Peace*, in Russian, read out loud with a British accent (so he sounded even smarter). I wanted him to shine so brightly that people would have to put on sunglasses.

But as I celebrated my father while holding my son in my

arms, I realized that I had actually been wanting way *too little* for Leo.

Now I realize that I want Leo to be like my father. I don't just want him to be happy, but also to make everyone around him happier. To not only be creative, but to make everyone around him more creative. To not only be successful, but to make everyone around him more successful. I don't just want him to be a bright light; I want him to make others shine brighter as well.

At the deepest heart of this research is my belief that there is no meaning in life without others. Think about it. The key to real leadership is inspiring others to be leaders. The key to good parenting, and strong relationships, is helping to bring out the best in the people we love. The key to true happiness is finding joy in helping others become happier. And the key to achieving your highest potential starts by helping others achieve theirs. I want that for Leo. And I want that for you, too.

It all starts with asking the bigger questions: How do I expand my influence in an interconnected world? How am I impacting others with my life and my energy? How do I raise my potential by making others better? I will argue that if you are not asking these questions, your potential is limited and your success will be short-lived. This book is an exploration of the new science showing how YOU can lift the ceiling on your own potential, well-being, and happiness by helping others do the same—making this a better, happier, and more prosperous world for all of us.

In these sometimes dark and complicated times, we don't need a lone light flashing in the night; we *need to shine brighter together*.

PART II

THE

SEEDS

OF

BIG

POTENTIAL

CHAPTER 3

SURROUND YOURSELF WITH POSITIVE INFLUENCERS

Creating Star Systems

In February 2014, my wife, Michelle, who was at the time eight months pregnant, told me that I was traveling too much and "suggested" I not accept any more work until after Leo was born. Then, as an afterthought, she added, "Unless, of course, Oprah calls." Three days later, Oprah's team called. A month later, I found myself sitting nervously in the backyard of Oprah's house in Montecito, California.

I had been invited for a one-hour interview for her show *Super Soul Sunday*, which honestly is the best show on television—a one-hour deep-dive interview with incredible thinkers from Brené Brown to Rob Bell. When I arrived, a film crew was setting up at the bottom of a path that wound through a redwood forest on her property. (Yes, she has a redwood forest, as one does.) There the cameras would capture the beautiful and natural moment where the guest—in this case me—meets Oprah for the first time. My moment was neither beautiful nor natural. As soon as I saw her, my brain shut off. I have tried to repress the memory of what happened next.

In her trademark singsong voice Oprah called out by way of greeting, "Shawn, Shawn, Shawn!" And that's when I realized I didn't know the protocol. How was I to reply? "Oprah, Oprah, Oprah"? So I brilliantly said . . . nothing. She had her hands raised, so I instinctively grabbed them, only to realize I had no idea whether this was a high five, a hug, or if we were about to dance. Unfortunately, what resulted was some horrendous hybrid of all three. Arms raised, hands clasped, we slowly began to spin awkwardly as my panicked eyes met her confused ones. After a few seconds and after rotating nearly 360 degrees, they mercifully shut off the cameras.

One of Oprah's gifts is making her guests feel so comfortable that they will want to reveal everything in a conversation with her—and I was no exception, even after my fiasco first encounter. Which is why the next part happened. After we taped the hour show, while her crew broke down the set, I revealed what I was feeling. I turned to Oprah and told her I was disappointed. I had loved our conversation, but there was something else I had really wanted to talk about: my experience having gone through depression. It is too easy to say, "Of course he is happy. He is a happiness researcher. He is married to a happiness researcher. His sister is a unicorn." Likewise, it's easy to think, "And of course Oprah is happy. Look at all her opportunities and resources and wealth and friends. Gotta be easy to be happy if you're Oprah."

Which is why I was so surprised by what happened next. Oprah turned to me and said, "Shawn, I went through two years of depression, at the height of my career, while making the most money, when *Beloved* did not do as well as I wanted to, and I shattered." I responded, "I went through two years of depression while I was at Harvard while teaching Harvard students how not to be depressed." She then signaled to the crew to turn the cameras back on and we ended up talking for a whole second hour about what to do when you have lost the joy somewhere in your pursuit of potential.

I tell you this story because what I learned from my struggle with depression is at the heart of this strategy, the first SEED of Big Potential. Back when I was at Harvard, I thought what I was doing was working. I had managed to get accepted into an Ivy League university after graduating from a public school in Waco. I got a full military scholarship. I graduated with high honors. I was so good at checking off these metrics of individual success that I never stopped to recognize that I was lonely and alone. I thought I could do everything by myself. And for a time I thought I *should* do everything by myself. That is, until I realized that not only was this mindset the root of my depression, it was also actually placing an invisible ceiling on my future success.

The turning point for me was when I changed my mindset from "I can do it all by myself" to "I need others." Depression taught me that to really achieve my Big Potential, I needed to surround myself with a stronger system. And that in order to make friends I had to *be* one first. So I picked up the phone. I reached out. I reconnected with people I cared about, and I went out of my way to listen to their problems—even if I myself was hurting.

But at the same time I had to be open about my challenges. All this time I had been trying to project an image of success, I had been too scared and ashamed to admit I needed help. But I soon realized that true connection is a two-way street—that "one-way friendships" actually make the system weaker and less resilient. So I dropped the act that everything was perfect and opened up to my twelve closest friends and family. I was going through depression, I told them, and I needed them. I stopped trying to be perfect and do everything "all by myself."

The impact was incredible. Not only did they immediately rally around me, but they also opened up about parts of their lives—like problems they struggled with, from loneliness to addiction—that had been hidden from me when my own pursuit of perfection made them feel I wasn't allowing them to be imperfect. This allowed me to get to know them on a deeper level than ever. The result was the best social support system that I had had in my twenty-four years of life up to that point. My depression broke, and I have since enjoyed more meaning and success than I ever could have achieved without that support system.

Sometimes, perhaps when surrounded by squabbling children, coughing plane passengers, or a negative and moody boss, we may long to escape to a secluded beach where we are the only person in the world. But while we all need periods of solitude from time to time in order to reflect and recharge, isolation is never the cure for what ails us in life. As human beings, we are wired to be tribal creatures rather than lone wolves; ever since the days of the hunter-gatherers we have desperately needed one another in order to survive. Indeed, all major religious traditions from Islam to Christianity to Judaism start in the same place: "Man is not meant to be alone."* Even

---

* I find it fascinating that this passage is so important it happens in the second chapter of the first book of the Bible. It is specifically in reference to Adam needing someone else in his life, but there is no indication that this is a gendered need. In fact, the rest of the scripture and traditions of Judaism, Christianity, and Islam all point to the fact that we need community and that at the heart of the religion is loving others.

in prison—one of the worst places in the world—the strongest form of punishment is putting someone in isolation.

And yet, ironically, at a time when technology and the Internet have enabled us to be more connected than at any other period in human history—a time when social networks allow us to communicate instantly and seamlessly with someone across the globe whom we have never met—I would argue that we are starving for real connection more than ever. And at the same time, we are only now beginning to understand the full impact that the networks of people around us have on our performance, well-being, happiness, and success.

If you've ever spent even five minutes on a trampoline, you have probably experienced what's called a "super bounce" (or a "double bounce"). When jumping on a trampoline alone, you can only jump so high. But if you convince someone to jump next to you—and you time it right—their extra weight augments the potential energy, and in turn you *both* spring up much higher. Big Potential is the super bounce that is possible only with others jumping with you.

The height of your potential is predicted by the people who surround you. So the key to creating a super bounce for your potential is to SURROUND yourself with people who will lift you up rather than drag you down. Because as you'll learn in this chapter, surrounding yourself with other elevated people can provide the energy needed to lift yourself to new heights.

Since that Oprah interview, I have had the opportunity to work with several Hollywood celebrities, famous athletes, and top executives who also suffer from feelings of loneliness and emptiness, despite their fame, success, and wealth. I've now concluded that there are three hidden costs to trying to be the brightest star shining alone: loneliness, loss of meaning, and eventual burnout. Pursuing potential individually does not lead to being a star for long. Just as stars collapse in upon themselves when they don't have a system around them, individuals trying to be superstars alone flame out and disappear before too long.

BE A SUPERSTAR WITHIN A CONSTELLATION OF STARS

I know you want to be a superstar. If you have kids, you want them to be superstars. I have seen countless parents send their kids to expensive private schools, hoping that the competitive atmosphere would turn them into superstar academics whom no school could turn down. Yet these hyper-competitive environments operate according to the misguided notion that in order to be "winners" there must be "losers" as well. This is simply not the case, and it completely misses the point of Big Potential. As famed basketball coach John Wooden once wrote, "The main ingredient of stardom is the rest of the team."

So let's get really real about winning. One of the most successful coaches in basketball, and perhaps in any sport, is Geno Auriemma, head coach of the UConn women's basketball team. As of the time of writing, Geno's team had not lost a game in two years, and his team had won the national championship four of the last five years. How does he do it? He cultivates a culture whereby players are judged by their contributions to the team rather than by their individual successes. Players who become stars by helping the whole team play better will get in the game, while those who try to be "superstars" by upstaging their teammates will sit on the bench. As Geno puts it: "I'd rather lose than watch kids play the way some kids play. . . . They're always thinking about themselves. Me, me, me, me. I didn't score, so why should I be happy? I'm not getting enough minutes, why should I be happy? . . . So when I watch game film, I'm checking what's going on on the bench. If somebody is asleep over there, if somebody doesn't care, if somebody's not engaged in the game, they will never get in the game. Ever."

You could put Geno on any team at any company and he would keep on winning, because his entire philosophy is to construct a team of stars rather than pamper a superstar. Similarly, Nick Saban, the venerated head coach of the University of Alabama's perennially championship-winning football team, doesn't buy into the tradition of handing out game balls to MVPs, because he believes that singling out players for individual achievements goes against his winning objective; for him, success is all about the team's win, not one superstar's stats. Unlike so many coaches, managers, and educators, both Geno and Nick know that a "me, me, me" attitude is toxic to a team—and the individual players on it.

In basketball, for example, you would think that shooting percentage would best predict the outcome of a game, right? But in fact a large BYU study found that the ratio of assists to turnovers is much more predictive of success.[1] That's because lots of turnovers means players are hogging the ball so that they can score, whereas lots of assists means the players aren't trying to make individual shots; they are trying to get the collective win.

In business, too, those who care only about their individual success won't get very far. Think of the hyper-competitive entrepreneur who stepped all over his cofounders, took advantage of his employees, and misled his investors—only to eventually run his company to the ground. Or think of the child actor who made her first million at age fourteen but is in rehab by sixteen, with the best days of her career behind her. Or the cocky athlete who wins his team the trophy one year, then is benched in year two for not playing well with others. All too often, we get so focused on showing off our individual strengths that we underestimate the greater strength that comes from the people we surround ourselves with.

In a fascinating study, Harvard researchers looked at a sample of 1,052 investment analysts who were competing at the top of their game. Things were going great for them. They had found a way to succeed in a tough and competitive job. They felt like superstars. Then the researchers looked at what happened when those analysts were moved to a new team at a new bank, or left for higher pay elsewhere. If success is all about the individual—individual grit, hard work, intelligence, and so forth—then those star analysts should have been able to perform equally well in their new environments and continue achieving unabated success. But that is not what happened. A whopping 46 percent of these stars collapsed. They simply were unable to replicate their successes at the new bank. And not just in the short term; the researchers found that FIVE years later, the analysts still could not perform at the level they once had. They stopped being superstars the minute they left behind the constellation of people who had allowed them to shine.

Even if you bring a ton of stars together, you have not necessarily created a winning team. One of the best examples is highlighted by Mark de Rond in an article for *Forbes*,[2] who describes how the soccer team Real Madrid spent 400 million euros (think about that for a moment) for the most incredible star cluster: Ronaldo, Beckham, Zindane, and the like. And then, from 2004 to 2006, one of the most expensive teams in soccer history had its worst seasons in team history. Meanwhile, between 2000 and 2006, the Oakland A's baseball team spent the least money of all the MLB teams in the draft, not splurging on superstar players, and yet won more games than almost any other team during that period. They might not have had the most star players, but they did have the best star system.

Companies (and schools) that systematically reward for individual achievement are actually undercutting their success rates, says Peter Kuhn, an economics professor at UC Santa Barbara. He and his team found that compensation programs based on individual performance created a "culture of back-stabbing and colleagues hoarding information from one another."[3] Men, he found, were especially likely to work individually toward their goals because they assumed that they were better than their peers. But when Kuhn teamed up with Marie Claire Villeval, an economics professor from the National Center for Scientific Research, they found that if you offered employees a 10 percent increase in pay to join a team instead of working individually, more men joined.[4] The male employees who were now incentivized to cooperate began to share more information and take time to train their colleagues, which helped improve the success of their teams. We need to move away from just rewarding individual work and incentivize making others better.

To do this we need to break the vicious cycle of a me, me, me mindset that we see infecting our society. We need to stop asking "How many points did you score?" and start asking **"How did you help your team win?"** We need to change our reward structures at work, home, and school. As Steve Kerr, a former chief learning officer at Goldman Sachs, wrote, "Leaders are hoping for A (collaboration) while rewarding B (individual achievement). They must instead learn how to spot and reward people who do both."[5]

Pursuing the collective win not only helps us perform better in the short term, it allows us to maintain resilience over time as well. The more we are interconnected, the more a single setback or negative event will be cushioned by other people. Similarly, the more people we have in our ecosystem to share stress, challenges, or burdens with, the lighter those burdens will be for each individual. Occasionally, superstar players will carry the team on their shoulders for the last two minutes before the clock runs out. But the only reason they have the strength to do so is that they shared in the energy expenditure throughout the game. In work, life, sports, or anywhere else, the way to win is to create a system in which members can assist each other, carry each other on their shoulders, and make each other better.

The conclusion of a decade of my work is clear. **You can be a superstar; you just can't be one alone.** What you need is a star system: **a constellation of positive, authentic influencers who support each other, reinforce each other, and make each other better.**

The people around us matter—a lot. And while we can't choose our family and we don't get to pick all the people we work with, we CAN strategically choose to SURROUND ourselves with people who will give us a super bounce rather than knock us down. In this chapter you'll learn how to *consciously craft your connections* to build a constellation of stars in which you can shine your brightest. It requires only three key steps:

STRATEGY #1: Tap into the power of positive peer pressure.

STRATEGY #2: Create balance through variety.

STRATEGY #3: Create reciprocal bonds.

In his brilliant book *The Short History of Nearly Everything,* Bill Bryson jokes that you are able to read his book only because all of your ancestors successfully procreated. While this is technically true, I think there's a corollary: You are reading this book because someone helped you learn to read.

Moreover, you are reading this book because someone inspired you to continue learning. Because someone showed you what it meant to be successful and you wanted to emulate it. Because someone taught you that you could reach your highest potential and then helped you acquire the tools you would need to get there.

In today's hyper-connected world, we need people like this more than ever. Which is why the first step in creating a star system is to seek out positive people who will inspire and teach us how to be better.

STRATEGY #1: TAP INTO THE POWER OF POSITIVE PEER PRESSURE

We know now that our individual traits are shaped by the people who SURROUND us. This is especially true in the workplace as the nature of work becomes more and more collaborative; as more and more companies move from closed-door offices to shared or open-plan workspaces, from phone calls to video-conferencing, from emails to messaging apps. Moreover, at a time when we have 24/7 access to social media and news feeds that are being refreshed literally every second, our exposure to other people's energy—positive or negative—is higher than ever. And the more of it we absorb, the more it impacts our motivation, our engagement, our performance, and our Big Potential.

We worry so much about negative peer pressure—whether from the toxic coworkers who infect us with their pessimism, the classmates constantly getting our kids into trouble, or the wealthy friends who pressure us into taking vacations we can't afford—that we often forget all about the power of **positive peer pressure**.

Just as being around negative, unmotivated people drains our energy and potential, surrounding ourselves with positive, engaged, motivated, and creative people causes our positivity, engagement, motivation, and creativity to multiply. In my work with companies, I created a formula to highlight the basic principle at the heart of this strategy:

Big Potential = Individual attributes x (positive influences - negative influences)

This isn't about networking with successful people to get ahead. Nor is it about surrounding yourself with people who always seem cheerful and happy. That's not what I mean by "positive." It's about surrounding yourself with people with positive traits who can "super bounce" your potential, and you theirs. Whereas negative influencers sap your energy, positive people actually *provide* energy when you are low, which helps you more effectively solve problems, deal with challenges, and work toward your goals. For example, I hired neuroscientist Brent Furl from Texas A&M to join our team, not just because he is a brilliant researcher but because we could meet for tennis and have conversations about spirituality. Having someone around you who meditates for two hours a day and who is a great athlete makes me want to meditate and exercise more—which is the positive peer pressure we are only beginning to understand through research.

For example, researchers at UPenn demonstrated how the influence of peers can affect us positively by creating "cascading mentoring" programs, ones in which college students teach computer skills to high school students, who then teach middle school students. In evaluating the program, the researchers found that simply observing how the cool college students have mastered the material makes the high schoolers eager to do the same; and in turn, the enthusiasm of the big high school students they idolize inspires the middle school students to study harder and learn more as well. In short, the very same social influences that might cause a teenager to drive more recklessly, skip class, or engage in various unsafe behaviors can be channeled toward "peer pressuring" that same teenager to want to learn.

In the workplace, positive peer pressure is so beneficial to the bottom line that some companies are either reversing or scaling back the telecommuting or remote-work policies that were so popular for many years. I suspect many of the readers of this book work remotely. I'm in the same boat; I give one hundred talks a year all over the world and travel to my clients for research, so I don't have an office unless you count my airplane seat. But in light of our new understanding of Big Potential, I'm working on putting an end to my telecommuting—and so are many giant companies from IBM to Yahoo, Aetna, and Bank of America.

Take, for example, IBM, which in 2017 stopped giving employees the option to work remotely. I find it fascinating that the company that not only led the telecommuting trend, but also gave us much of the technology to make it possible, has completely reversed course. IBM famously championed the idea of remote working once they realized it would allow them to reduce their office space by seventy-eight million square feet— and sell that space for a $1.9 billion gain.[6] At one point, 40 percent of IBM workers could work from home or remotely. They even championed research that said working from home was a good idea. But now they have come to the conclusion that people work faster, are more creative, and are more collaborative when they are surrounded by others.[7] This is not an inconsequential decision. First of all, office space is expensive. Second, people like working from home, which means the company will likely lose talent, which is expensive to replace.

While conventional wisdom assumes that you work more hours when you work remotely (because there is no end to the day), new research has found that the marginal increase in productivity doesn't compare to the innovation, creativity, social connection, engagement, and company loyalty we pick up from our peers just by being in the same physical space. When asked how many people telecommute at Google, their CFO replied, "As few as possible."[8] In the modern world, our limiting factor is not how much we do; it is how little we meaningfully connect.

Moreover, running with a positive group of people at work can make you more positive, and Gallup found that positive and engaged workers make 60 percent fewer errors, have 49 percent fewer accidents, and have a much lower—67 percent lower— rate of absenteeism. Not to mention they are far more pleasant to be around, which means that everyone—from colleagues to clients to those looser but no less important connections— wants to work and do business with them.

If positivity and optimism are "contagious," it stands to

reason that there are also myriad benefits to surrounding yourself with Positive Influencers in your personal life. Research on optimistic men not only found that they enjoyed their relationships more, but their wives reported greater levels of relationship happiness as well.[9] Optimistic parents more often than not raise optimistic kids—who will, in turn, be fantastic positive influences on their own peers (remember that the effects of social contagion begin as early as age three). Optimists handle relationship crises better, they are more involved and nurturing parents,[10] and they are more resilient. Research on mothers from Mexico found that optimism was a predictor of the ability to cope with economic stress upon arriving in the United States.[11] When bad things happen, such as the loss of a job for an extended period of time, Positive Influencers are able to maintain higher life satisfaction.[12]

Given how contagious negativity is, surrounding yourself with optimists is like giving yourself a flu shot against stress and apathy. Thus, our very first task is to seek out positive people who help us sharpen our tools and build our strengths, both at work and in life. Before passing away, Jim Rohn, the wildly successful motivational author, built his business on the idea that "you are the average of the five people you spend the most time with." Who are the five people you spend the most time with? Now make a very quick Venn diagram of your life with three circles: Who leaves me feeling good? Who strengthens me? Who makes me hope for more? Which of your five people fit into all three categories? These are your Positive Influencers. Most likely, these will be people who are self-aware, open, compassionate, present, resilient, and optimistic.

There is the famous line "A happy wife is a happy life." But so is a happy child, a happy best friend, a happy office mate, a happy boss—they just don't rhyme neatly. The key is to **seek people who bring out the best in you, not the stress in you**.

And there are actually benefits to surrounding yourself with positive people even if you don't know them personally. I was introverted for certain parts of my life, so when I would move to a new city where I had not yet made new friends, I brought my Positive Influencers with me: authors such as C. S. Lewis, Hermann Hesse, Brandon Sanderson, and Patrick Rothfuss. **You are what you read.** And science confirms this. Researchers from Dartmouth and Ohio State found that when you become engrossed with a book you may actually begin to not just identify with, but actually take on some of the traits and characteristics of, the main character.[13] For example, if you read a book about someone with a strong social conscience, your likelihood of doing something socially conscientious rises. Of course, this phenomenon has one drawback; I used to love watching shows like *Breaking Bad*, but to be honest, I didn't feel like as good a person afterward. I now find myself not wanting to enter fictional worlds that glorify the negative, because I find that they have real-world ramifications on my mood and self-image. Instead, I gravitate toward things that make me feel stronger, smarter, and better, not angry, disillusioned, and reactive.

So whenever possible, you should strive to surround yourself with books, magazines, and other forms of the written word that uplift and inspire, instead of those that invite negativity into your life. The same holds true for the music and podcasts you carry around with you on your phone: Are the people constantly speaking to you through your headphones and speakers positive, optimistic, and kind? The more you surround yourself with positive voices, the easier positive change will be to sustain and even amplify.

STRATEGY #2: CREATE BALANCE THROUGH VARIETY

When Michelle and I got married, I bought my wedding ring on Amazon.com for $15. Then I bought my replacement wedding ring for $15 on Amazon. I mention this to give you a mental image to contrast with the ring I wear on my other hand: a $150 ring I designed for myself with the money I earned for winning my fantasy football league. Crowned with surely authentic "diamonds," stamped with "Shawn" on one side and "Genius" on the other, and inscribed with flowing letters on the inside—it is a stunning monument to obnoxiousness, especially as it cost literally ten times what my wedding ring did.

For all of you who have never played fantasy football, I'll give you the basics. During the draft, your goal is to fill out your team with a variety of players and positions: a quarterback, some running backs and wide receivers, a tight end, a kicker, and some defense. This reflects the reality in sports; a team made up of all superstar quarterbacks can't carry out even a single play, much less win the game. We already know that in sports as in life, you can't be a superstar alone. This leads us to a simple but often overlooked principle that applies as much to fantasy sports as it does to your network of Positive Influencers: the more varied and diverse your team, the better.

From evolutionary theory, we know that the key to survival is biodiversity. The more diverse the genetic makeup of a species, the more resilient they are in the face of disease and other forces of nature. By the same token, the more diverse your social support network, the more resilient you will be when life throws you a curveball. So we need to take a moment to mentally check the genetic makeup of our relationships. Are you surrounded only by people just like you—by people of the same race, gender, political beliefs, interests, and ambitions? If so, you are limiting your potential and your growth.

But diversity isn't just about things like age, gender, or even what you do for a living. In one fascinating study described in *Harvard Business Review,* Alison Reynolds and David Lewis tested six teams using a mathematical model that measured their "cognitive diversity"—essentially, how differently or similarly they thought. Two people might hail from two completely different cultures or work in two completely different fields but think in similar ways, or two people might have grown up in the same town and both work in the same industry but think worlds apart. As it turned out, the most cognitive diversity, the better; not only did the teams with the most cognitive diversity have the highest performance scores, the bottom two groups for diversity actually failed the performance measures.[14]

Many teams and companies are reluctant to pursue diversity for fear of relationship conflict or friction; they assume that people who are too different from one another will struggle to work together collaboratively. Yet another study summarized in *Harvard Business Review* found not only that these fears were exaggerated, but that bringing an "outsider" onto a largely homogenous team actually doubled the team's chances of solving a challenging problem, and that this happened precisely *because* the relationship produced friction.[15] While people perceive collaboration as more challenging when teams are diverse, the researchers concluded that adding cognitive diversity leads to better outcomes because it forces people to stretch out of their comfort zones and consider perspectives and ideas they might not have considered, or even agree with.

The research on cognitive diversity has always made me wonder: What if we took standardized tests such as the SAT,

LSAT, GRE, or GMAT as a group rather than alone? When I suggest this to people, everyone immediately worries that less smart people taking the test with them will lower their score (which is humorous, because statistically, for at least 50 percent of the test takers, the other person would improve their score). But since people have different cognitive strengths, might you do better if you were paired with people who balanced out your skills? Some would argue that the entire point of standardized testing is to measure your individual aptitude, but since we now know that individual performance on a test is actually a very poor predictor of whether you would succeed in college or grad school, why bother with individualized testing? Wouldn't solving problems with a group of people be more representative of most work you would do with an advanced degree in the real world?

The more diverse your ecosystem, the stronger and more resilient it is. By letting in influences that previously were missing, much like the wolves who were introduced into Yellowstone, we can better protect ourselves against threats. Moreover, the more diverse your network, the better you will be able to engineer serendipity. In *The Luck Factor,* Dr. Richard Wiseman argues that the key to "luck" is to vary your relationships and routines so that you have access to new ideas and possibilities. Having too many similar people in your network means you're leaving all kinds of doors unopened and all kinds of opportunities unutilized. If you have twelve good friends at work and they are all in accounting, for example, you're never going to hear about that job opening in the marketing department, or get invited to work on that big initiative with the project development team.

But it's not enough to cultivate a star system of diverse people; you also want to choose people who serve diverse *purposes* in your life. To do so, I suggest seeking a mix of three types of Positive Influencers: **pillars, bridges, and extenders.**

Pillars are those who are a rock for you in tough times. These are the people who have your back regardless: the loyal best friend who will drop everything to come over late at night bearing ice cream, the mentor at work who will champion you for the promotion or big account, the teammate who will pick up your slack when you are overextended or struggling to keep your head above water. You should have plenty of other people in your life who push you and call you on things, but you also need sources of unconditional support and acceptance.

Bridges are connectors to new people or resources outside of your existing ecosystem. A bridge might be the person to invite you into a club or committee or basketball league, or they might be one to introduce you to investors who might be interested in funding your project. You'll know someone is a bridge if their connections and resources do not overlap entirely with yours. And note that a person doesn't necessarily have to be of higher status to be a bridge to high-potential people or opportunities.

One of the biggest mistakes people make is to focus too heavily on the traditional hierarchy when looking for new connections or new perspectives. I saw the dangers of this firsthand when I worked with a large merchandiser whose senior leadership was struggling to improve the efficiency of their pre-ship warehouse—a place, I was shocked to discover, that some of the heads of strategy and consumer affairs had never visited. So I suggested a visit to the warehouse, and it was stunning how many creative ideas the warehouse managers gave the leaders to take back to corporate headquarters. Once the executives looked beyond the official hierarchy and recognized the managers at the warehouse as being experts with enormous insight into day-to-day operations, they became much more equipped to solve the complex logistical problems facing their business.

Just as good ideas can come from anywhere, access to opportunities is not just about being best friends with people in high places. In the 1960s, sociologist Mark Granovetter wrote a paper based on his research into how people found jobs. Repeatedly he found that it wasn't close friends; it was actually just acquaintances who helped them land their jobs.[16] Adding a few more weak ties to your network, regardless of those connections' status, increases your potential to transform an opportunity into a reality.

Extenders are Positive Influencers who push you out of your comfort zone. This could take the form of a mentor or a friend who has a skill set or personality very different from yours. For example, I'm on the shy and introverted side, so I need my extraverted friends to help set up social engagements and get me to try new experiences. And as someone who tends to multitask and pursue many projects at once, I need my more focused and detailed-oriented friends to slow me down when I'm racing roughshod toward a goal.

We often find ourselves attracted to people just like us, which leads to an echo chamber that limits our exposure not only to different ideas and perspectives but also to new and different experiences. Doctors who socialize only with other doctors, for example, might never get out of their comfort zones to go to art or cooking classes. Sports fanatics who hang out only with other sports fanatics might never get out of their comfort zones to go to the symphony. Indeed, research shows that capitalizing on diversity requires embracing people's differences—*especially* when doing so causes discomfort or feels threatening.

The key to leadership is not planning and positioning; it is people. When Jim Collins and his research team studied outstanding business leaders, they expected that the good-to-great transformational leaders they had selected would start with vision and strategy. Instead, they found that the leaders "attended to people first, strategy second." As a leader, your performance is interconnected with that of the people on your team; the more diverse that team is, the better.

So starting today, for the next week, make it a point to talk to someone you wouldn't have talked to in your sphere—whether it is a simple "How are you doing?" or making a lunch or coffee date. Make an effort to walk toward anyone you have a tendency to try to avoid by putting your cellphone up to your ear. And try to take the time to get to know people who push you out of your comfort zone: people who are "different," not just in terms of race or gender, but who *think* differently as well. This could be the woman on your team who always comes up with the wacky but "just crazy enough to work" ideas, the relative with political beliefs you don't agree with, or the elderly neighbor with a unique background and life experiences. The lesson at the heart of this strategy is that we have something to learn from everyone, as long as we can learn to truly listen to and connect with them.

And finally, try to help those in your ecosystem connect with others as well. Random network theory demonstrates that "as the average number of links per node in our network increases beyond the critical one, the number of nodes left out of the giant cluster decreases exponentially."[17] **That is, the more connections we add to our network, the harder it is to find a node that remains isolated.** Every time we help people around us increase the breadth and variety of people in their life—even by getting to know just one more person—we dramatically strengthen the entire system. The more nodes you have, the less chance there is of someone falling through the cracks, and thus the greater your resilience in tough times. Remember that biodiversity is the lifeblood of our relationships, and that the stronger and more diverse your network, the more support you'll have in achieving your Big Potential.

STRATEGY #3: CREATE RECIPROCAL BONDS

Earlier I described how during the time I was suffering with depression I needed to lower my walls and truly let people in. One-way relationships do not give you the "super bounce" of energy to build or sustain potential for long. You know what I'm talking about when I say "one-way friend." These are those people in your life who want to tell you all about their relationship problems or what's frustrating them at work, but when you need them they are uninterested or absent. By the same token, it's up to you not to be that person to your colleagues, family, and friends. Instead, you want to find a balance between baring your true self and being a good listener when others bare theirs. The best relationships are built on reciprocal bonds: the final key to a good Star System.

It's tempting to reach out to people in our networks only when we need something, but to get the most out of the relationship, we should make a habit of reaching out to offer something to them. As Robert Cross from UVA found, "Reciprocal relationships also tend to be more fruitful; the most successful leaders always look for ways to give more to their contacts."[18] If you want to go deeper on this topic, there's no reason to reinvent the wheel. Adam Grant's book *Give and Take* is the best place to learn how helping others helps you. "When takers win," he wrote, "there's usually someone else who loses. Research shows that people tend to envy successful takers and look for ways to knock them down a notch. In contrast, when givers . . . win, people are rooting for them and supporting them, rather than gunning for them. Givers succeed in a way that creates a ripple effect, enhancing the success of people around them."

The more reciprocal the relationship, the more impact it has on our happiness, engagement, and creativity. In one study, researchers evaluated the impact of real friends versus fake friends on our well-being and happiness. When two individuals labeled each other as a friend, it was considered a "mutual friendship," but if only one of them did, it was euphemistically called a "perceived friendship." The researchers found that if a nearby mutual friend was happy, a person's likelihood of being happy as well increased by 63 percent. If a nearby *perceived* friend was happy, however, that person had only a 12 percent chance of being happy.[19] In my opinion, there is actually something quite sad about a "perceived friendship."

Reciprocal bonds also foster psychological safety, which Google's Project Aristotle study concluded to be the key ingredient to a team's success—and one that matters much more than individual traits such as creativity, grit, or intelligence. Harvard Business School professor Amy Edmondson defines psychological safety as a "shared belief held by members of a team that the team is safe for interpersonal risk-taking." When relationships on a team are a two-way street, it instills what Edmondson describes as "a sense of confidence that the team will not embarrass, reject, or punish someone for speaking up." A climate of trust and mutual respect, where everyone feels comfortable being themselves, is a critical ingredient for any team striving for Big Potential.

This strategy has just one pitfall to watch out for: collaborative overload. When pursuing Big Potential, it's easy to become tempted to rack up as many connections as we possibly can. But when those relationships are two-way streets—that is, we put in what we get out of them—we can run the risk of overextending ourselves. In spite of what most self-help books say, research shows that individuals who simply know a lot of people are less likely to achieve standout performance, because they're spread too thin.[20] This is particularly true of high-achieving people, simply because the more successful you become, the more people will want your time.

Similarly, Adam Grant recently coauthored a thought-provoking piece for *Harvard Business Review* with Rob Cross and Reb Rebele in which they found in a study of more than 300 organizations that up to a third of value-adding collaborations came from 3 to 5 percent of the individuals. It makes sense: Once someone becomes known for being an amazing collaborator, everyone wants to collaborate with them. It may seem like a good thing to be in such high demand, but in fact the researchers found that when the number of colleagues demanding one's time rose to twenty-five people or more, job satisfaction and happiness plummeted. They wrote, "We find that as the percentage of requesters seeking more access [to the excellent collaborator] moves beyond about 25, it hinders the performance of both the individual and the group and becomes a strong predictor of voluntary turnover."

I've experienced this myself. I used to accept every invitation to give a talk, take every call for "a potential partnership," and sign on for every research proposal, and I loved all of it.

Then, suddenly, it reached a tipping point where I felt like I was so overcommitted that I couldn't get through a morning without letting several people down—and I'm a people pleaser, so that killed me. As we are seeking Big Potential, we need to limit our exposure to "collaborative overload" by not trying to be everything to everyone, and being strategic about whom we form connections with.

One of my former students and good friends once ran to be the student president of Harvard. His humility and humor made him wildly popular, but because he was involved in so many collaborations to improve the university, he got overextended and his grades and work started to falter. The further behind he got, the more he pushed off deadlines to later in the semester, and in turn the more behind he fell. What saved him in the end was exactly what saved me in my battle with depression: He let people in. Once he opened up to his professors and let them know what he was going through, they found enough compassion and understanding for his situation that they gave him lots of leeway. So often we run ourselves ragged trying to be the superstar, but strong relationships allow us to achieve the same success without the cost of loneliness, alienation, and burnout.

We need reciprocal bonds in order to create a Star System we can truly shine in. To find people who are willing to be open, authentic, and giving, the greatest test is whether you are willing and able to be open, authentic, and giving yourself. And if you do find those super bouncers, hold tight because they are golden. The result will be not only greater potential for you but deeper and more meaningful relationships.

GRAY TOWN

Those of you who know me well know that my favorite author and intellectual idol is C. S. Lewis, a man who possessed the rare ability to have complex theological discussions with the dons of Oxford while making that same theology meaningful to a six-year-old in his fiction writing. While I love all of his writing, the most influential work of Lewis on my own writing has been *The Great Divorce,* which is a short novel about people who are in purgatory after dying—or what he calls living in the Gray Town. At first the people in the gray town all lived in close proximity, but as challenges and struggles arose in the community, people built new homes farther away. Once they felt like that new home was too close to that nosy neighbor, or that "negative" friend, or that person who didn't call them back last week, they would move a little bit farther away. And then farther and then farther. Pretty soon every little petty disagreement or perceived slight caused them to move farther and farther apart. As a result, the people in heaven saw the Gray Town as a type of hell where people experienced only darkness, isolation, distrust, and loneliness. I thought this was an apt perspective on a hell.

I once had a friend who often told me that she liked talking to me because I was positive. At first I was flattered, but then as I got to know her better, she also seemed to have a lot of stories about people at work who were negative or backbiting or gossipy or toxic. Or waiters who were intentionally avoiding her, lazy ex-boyfriends who never respected her, or friends who were jealous of her. We once went on a trip together, during which she had an altercation with a guy on the plane who didn't let her out of her seat when we landed, got upset because she thought the travel agent who couldn't change our flight was being rude, and called the hotel manager about how noisy the maids were in the hall. In isolation, each of these things seems fairly normal and rational to be upset about. Yes, the maids were loud. Yes, the travel agent could have been nicer. Yes, the guy should have let her out of her row first. But taken all together it was clear she had a pattern of letting small negative things turn into big things and ignoring the positives in the relationship or in the situation. As a result she was distancing herself from her coworkers, friends, lovers, and family. She was not only slowly dismantling her social ecosystem, she was creating her own private hell.

I use that word because it's loaded, and because I know how awful it can be when you feel so alone and disconnected from the world, having gone through depression for two years myself. Depression is a Gray Town. And ironically, the best ticket out of the Gray Town is the very thing we often push away: social connection. Everyone we know has flaws and imperfections, and if you look for reasons to feel disappointed, alienated, or frustrated, those reasons are not hard to find. For me, depression was a symptom of my physical, emotional, and spiritual disconnect from others. Even Oprah, who has more material success than anyone, was not immune to depression and the momentary eclipse of meaning. When this happens, we need people around us more than ever. As Helen Schucman once wrote, and which later appeared in *A Course in Miracles*, "Your task is not to seek for love, but merely to seek and find all the barriers within yourself that you have built against it."

Everyone needs occasional moments of solitude, but true meaning, success, and happiness are impossible unless we are connected to others. Big Potential reminds us that only by surrounding ourselves with other stars are we able to truly shine.

CHAPTER 4

EXPAND YOUR POWER

Leading from Every Seat

"I SAVED A LIFE"

In December 2016, I was driven out in the middle of nowhere in Northern California on a cold, wet morning. Bewildered as to why we were venturing so far out from the city, I checked Google Maps more and more frequently as cows began replacing Starbucks. Then I lost cell service. Finally, the car stopped in front of what appeared to be an old mill. To my surprise, the inner building and grounds that had once served a much different capacity had been transformed into a venue for life-affirming events such as weddings and reunions. This stark makeover seemed symbolic of the reason I was there: to learn about a new program at Kaiser Permanente that had transformed receptionists and other support staff into lifesaving medical providers. As of our meeting, this program had saved 471 lives.

In the room generally reserved for brides and their entourage,

I had the honor of meeting with Dr. Sanjay Marwaha and Monica Azevedo from the Permanente Medical Group, who told me about the program titled "I Saved a Life." Its approach was as straightforward as it was innovative: to empower all hospital employees—even people without medical training—to provide medical care. I know what you're thinking: "Here comes a malpractice suit." But hear me out.

In a Small Potential organization, there are very clear mental compartments about who is capable of leading change. Stifled by layers of hierarchy, such organizations create a false dichotomy between those with the power to decide, innovate, or act and those who must blindly follow. In the case of the medical industry, it is too easy to conceive of doctors and nurses as "medical providers" and the administrators and receptionists as "support staff." This seems, at first glance, like a perfectly logical way to go about delineating tasks in a hospital setting. But as we'll see, this type of thinking limits our ability to tap into Big Potential.

Imagine you have an earache. You go to your primary doctor. After you wait half an hour in the examination room, he swoops in, takes a peek inside your ears, and then refers you to an ENT specialist. You make an appointment for your ears, fill out a bunch of paperwork about your ears, the doctor asks about your ears, and you pay the receptionist for your ear exam. All of this seems normal because you have a problem with your ears.

But what if your earache is actually caused by a virus that you caught because the anxiety that is keeping you up at night had weakened your immune system? After all, you are an interconnected organism, and there are any number of other things happening in your brain and body at any given moment that could be causing you to experience pain in your ear. But because your ENT specializes in ears, she might not think to ask you about your mood or your sleep patterns, and fail to get at the root cause of the pain in your ear. In a world in which medical providers are becoming more and more specialized and siloed into smaller and smaller domains, the team at Kaiser wondered, how can we step back and see the bigger picture?

The answer they came up with was quite simple: They would upend the false dichotomy that governs most hospitals in the world, and empower those outside the traditional role of "medical provider" to address health issues that might slip through the cracks of a highly hierarchical organization. Knowing that one of the most effective, and yet underutilized, tools for improving health outcomes is preventive care, the team at Kaiser decided to invite and train receptionists to find ways to increase the number of patients who took advantage of preventive care options.

Now, if you called to book an appointment for any reason—even for an earache—the call center representative could first check to see if you are overdue for a preventive screening (mammogram, cervical, or colorectal) and then ask if you would like to book an appointment. The beauty of this program is that Kaiser empowered anyone who is involved in overseeing, providing, or scheduling care—medical degree or no medical degree—to contribute to the core objective of the organization: improving patients' health.

And boy did it work. If a patient agrees to be booked for a screening and a life-threatening cancer is found in time to be treated, that is considered a life saved. When Kaiser Permanente tracked the outcomes, they found that of the 1,179 women who had been diagnosed with breast cancer in their hospitals since the new program began, a whopping 40 percent had booked that mammogram at the suggestion of one of the nonmedical staff through the "I Saved a Life" program. One life saved would have made the program worthwhile. Four hundred and seventy-one lives saved is transformative.

If I asked you which employees you would expect to be among the greatest heroes in the hospital, you probably wouldn't think of receptionists—a group of people who don't ever step foot in the operating room, who don't take blood, read X-rays, or even see patients face-to-face. And these heroes are often sitting in a call center chair surrounded by cubicle walls, which means that in order to persuade a patient to come in for their screening, they have to rely on emotional connection, data, and storytelling, all over the phone. And to do this effectively first and foremost requires they *believe* that they have the power to make an impact: to be able to say "*I* saved a life."

The ultimate key to the program's success was that it allowed anyone to be a leader regardless of job title, college degree, or years of experience. In other words, they created a system where people could lead from every seat.

No matter what field you are in or what type of work you do, believing that you, too, can lead from any seat multiplies your potential to create change. People who try to be superstars alone, who believe that they have the power to create change only if and when they occupy an "official" leadership role, will achieve only Small Potential. But when everyone in a system, no matter their official role or position, shares the work of creating change, there is virtually no limit to what can be achieved. **We need to free ourselves from the tyranny of labels if we are to achieve Big Potential.**

So many people believe that leadership is an individual sport—a burden to be shouldered alone. **Yet, trying to carry all the leadership responsibility alone is the quickest path to**

burnout. If you were running a hospital ward and you thought the outcome of each and every patient was on your shoulders alone, you might feel compassion fatigue. Similarly, if you were a sales manager or CFO who thought you had to bear the sole responsibility for your company's returns to its shareholders, you'd be crushed by an enormous weight. If as a parent you felt like you had to make all the decisions about your teen's future, you would be creating an undue, unnecessary, and unhelpful relationship stress. Think about how often high-potential leaders have been told, "If you want the job done right you have to do it yourself." This is not only untrue, it's the fastest way to put a cap on what you can achieve. Your time and energy are finite, but the demands on them are infinite. You simply cannot meet those demands unless you EXPAND responsibility and the work of leadership to everyone who has a stake in the mission.

In the introduction of this book, I described research coming out of neuroscience and positive psychology revealing the exorbitant cost to individuals and organizations when we treat success as a zero-sum game. The same is true with leadership. If you believe that leadership and influence are limited resources given only to those at the very top, it shuts off the part of your brain that could be searching for new possibilities or opportunities to lead. This cognitive meltdown not only prevents you from seeing the ways in which you *do* have the power to create change, it dramatically lowers your energy, creativity, happiness, and ultimate effectiveness. If we want small potential we should leave leadership in the hands of the "leaders." If we want Big Potential we must inspire and enable others to lead from every seat. When you let go of the idea that only certain people have the power to lead, you can dramatically amplify not only your own power but also the power of the group as a whole.

district was toxic and hopeless, and he would surely burn out and become completely disillusioned by his chosen career path before he even gotten started on it. But Joel was an optimist, and he did not think that the narrative of Cardinal he was hearing was the right one. He believed that if you could get everyone in an ecosystem to buy into the idea that they have the power to create meaningful change, you could raise the potential and performance of the entire system, and every individual in it.

He accepted the job as superintendent. That year, while walking through a Barnes & Noble store, Joel noticed a book with an obnoxious orange cover. It was mine. He began reading *The Happiness Advantage*, which validated the approach he wanted to take at Cardinal, and he immediately began instituting positive changes as superintendent. Joel knew that in order to raise his own potential as a leader, he needed all the help he could get. So the very first thing he did was identify whom he needed to surround himself with—the Positive Influencers within the community. He found the teachers who were positively engaged and who still believed in the power of education, and he promoted those leaders to the heads of each of the important school committees. Then, with their help, he set out to change hearts and minds throughout the ecosystem.

When most people think about who holds the power in schools, they tend to make the mistake of thinking only about teachers, principals, and superintendents. But when Joel thought about who the powerful people at Cardinal were, his list included not just the teachers and administration but also the cafeteria staff, the librarians, the janitors, and the crossing guards. Most schools offer occasional training for their teachers and top administrators, but rarely if ever does the leadership training extend to other, equally important, members of the staff: the student-facing employees like the bus drivers, the maintenance workers, and the receptionists in the principal's office. He would have to empower the people in these seats to lead; but first, he knew, he had to help them recognize that they were leaders.

So he made a pitch to everyone working at the school district, telling them that each and every one of them, no matter their official role, job function, or pay grade, could have a dramatic impact on not only the school's culture but on the very future of the students. He then turned those words into action. He encouraged the bus drivers to write personal notes to brighten the day of each of the individual kids who took their bus. He invited the substitute teachers to join the teacher trainings. He created workshops to teach the lunch staff about the benefits of positivity. In short, he set out to empower everyone in his Star System to be superstars.

The changes were already starting to have an effect, but Joel knew that in order to sustain and maintain the initial momentum, he needed to get people to buy into this cultural shift. It was at that time that a flyer, once again printed in an obnoxious shade of orange, caught Joel's eye. It was an advertisement for a public workshop AASA, The School Superintendents Association, was having on positive psychology and a parable I wrote called *The Orange Frog*.

The *Orange Frog* parable was initially a children's book I wrote, mostly for fun, on a long flight back from Australia. Many parents had written in to my company's website saying that they wished there were a way to get the concepts of *The Happiness Advantage* into children's hands long before they were able to read a book full of scientific research. My goal for the book was to invent a story, one that would be fun and easy for kids to read, about someone who feared that being positive made them different, but in the end found out how advantageous it was to be an optimist.

The book is about a frog named Spark who lives on an island populated by green frogs; Spark is an outcast among them because he has one orange spot. In addition to his strange coloration, Spark is an optimist surrounded by pessimists, and the more Spark does to spread his positivity to those other frogs, the more orange he becomes, causing him to be even more of a pariah on the island. Over the course of the book, Spark finds that his orange coloring is not only advantageous in protecting him from the predators in his ecosystem (the herons, obviously), but also contagious, and he begins finding ways of turning the other frogs orange. The purpose of the parable, of course, was to show how a single positive person could end up creating a ripple effect of positivity that infects those around him.

Joel soon realized that he wanted to create a similar ripple effect at the Cardinal Community School District—one that would infect all the "green frogs" working at the schools with the belief that they were leaders, and that each and every one of them possessed the power to help the struggling students reach their fullest potential. So Joel adopted the *Orange Frog* workshop as the narrative around which he would rally everyone at Cardinal.

The ripple effects were beautiful. Not only were bus drivers and teachers and lunch staff all reading the book, they soon adopted a graphic novel version of *The Orange Frog* we created so that entire classrooms could read the book together. The students soon began to own the change by creating random-acts-of-kindness clubs, where they would go out and do thoughtful things for students who needed a pick-me-up. Staff and students alike started practicing gratitude, mediation, and journaling. Whether their seat was on the faculty, on the janitorial or cafeteria staff, or behind the desk in a classroom, and whether they had advanced degrees in education or merely a high school diploma, these orange frogs became true agents of change. (You can watch a fantastic video of the Cardinal intervention at shawnachor.com, where you can see previously disengaged teachers running around and changing the complexion of the school from threat level red to a bright, brilliant orange.)

When I work with schools across the nation, so many have inspiring anecdotal stories of teachers who made a difference in the lives of their students. What makes Cardinal different, however, is that they had data, allowing them to actually quantify the impact of getting people to lead from every seat. Since 2012, average ACT scores at Cardinal High School increased from **17 to 21 in just a five-year period of time!** And in 2016 Cardinal boasted a 92 percent graduation rate; this would be an impressive achievement at any school, but for a poorly funded district once called a "failure factory," it is truly extraordinary. Joel himself is a superstar educator, but instead of carrying all that weight of change on his shoulders, he expanded it across a Star System that shone infinitely brighter than he could have alone.

Due to the changes that Joel and his team implemented, enrollment at Cardinal High began to rise for the first time in decades. Parents who could have chosen to send their kids to schools in the richest districts were actually picking the school in the poorest county because they believed it would give their kids a better education. Finally, the county elected to pass a $5.3 million bond to further invest in the positive momentum at their schools, and today the successes from Cardinal are being replicated at schools across Iowa, Arizona, Wisconsin,

Michigan, Kentucky, and Illinois. In Illinois, for example, Schaumburg School District 54 already had among the highest achievement scores in the state, but Superintendent Andy DuRoss believed that they could unlock even more of their students' potential if they could get the entire ecosystem operating on the same positive frequency. So, in April, he and Principal Amanda Stochl took the *Orange Frog* research to the staff, faculty, and every student at Lincoln Prairie School. After just twenty-one days, they found that 91 percent of students felt happier at school, 70 percent felt happier outside of school, and 85 percent believed they could still learn to be happier. And, a full 96.3 percent of staff and faculty felt more positive at the end of the three-week journey.

Joel and other educators like him were able to transform their school districts against all odds, not just because they recognized their own power to effect change, but because they understood how to *expand* that power to turn those around them into true change makers.

In this chapter you'll learn how to do the same, by following four key strategies:

> STRATEGY #1: Lead from the eleventh chair.
>
> STRATEGY #2: Develop your Elevated Pitch.
>
> STRATEGY #3: Use progress as fuel.
>
> STRATEGY #4: Lead from every lunch seat.

STRATEGY #1: LEAD FROM THE ELEVENTH CHAIR
(RECOGNIZE YOUR ABILITY TO LEAD)

Benjamin Zander, the conductor of the Boston Philharmonic Orchestra, has been nominated for multiple Grammys, and has given a popular TED Talk on music and passion.[1] In his talk, he tells the story of a cellist who was feeling discouraged that she was the eleventh chair in the cello section.[2] Instead of focusing on the fact that she was part of one of the best and most famous orchestras in the world, all she could focus on was the ten people in the chairs ahead of her. Despite the incredible talent she must have had to even be able to join such an elite organization, she felt like she was a lowly cog in the wheel.

Sensing her disengagement, Zander decided to ask her how she thought he should conduct a very challenging section of the symphony they were to perform the following week. She cautiously offered her opinion, and the very next week Zander conducted the piece just as she had suggested, to rave reviews. As Zander tells it, "From then on, this cellist who sat in the eleventh seat played like a completely different person." Why? In his talk, Zander describes how the cellist told him that it was because she now felt like a leader, even from the bottom of the organizational hierarchy of the orchestra, at her lowly eleventh chair. What I love about this story of potential is that not only did that eleventh-chair cellist raise her performance to new heights, so did the entire orchestra. This kind of harmony is the goal of Big Potential. And to achieve it, we must empower people to lead, no matter what chair they are in.

We can all achieve similar harmony in our lives and work once we expand the limited definition of leadership that still prevails in most businesses, schools, and organizations. In the 2014 Global Human Capital Trends survey from consulting firm Deloitte, the need for "leaders at all levels" was found to be one of the most critical issues facing today's companies,[3] with 86 percent of respondents rating it "urgent" or "important." In a paper examining the findings, leaders from Deloitte wrote that cultivating leadership at every level "remains the No. 1 talent issue facing organizations around the world."[4] And yet, only 13 percent of respondents say they do a good job of developing leaders at all levels, indicating a massive readiness gap that foretells a bleak future if we don't quickly empower everyone—regardless of rank, age, or job title—to step up and lead.

The old definition of potential (that is, Small Potential) is based on the myth that unless you are in a formal position of authority or power, you cannot change other people and you cannot change a culture. But while this myth is all too widely endorsed among the business and education communities (even a 2016 cover of *Harvard Business Review* asserted that "you can't fix culture"), the truth is that this kind of change IS possible.[5]

But you must first **recognize that you can create change wherever YOU are**. If you're an eleventh-chair cellist, you can offer your conductor suggestions that will elevate the performance of the entire orchestra. If you're a student, you can shift the mood of the entire classroom for good or bad. If you are a middle manager, you can change how people you lead treat their kids after work by creating a culture of support instead of stress. If you are a "lowly" intern or assistant, you can set your boss up for a more productive client meeting by emailing the documents to everyone a day in advance. At Kaiser Permanente, the receptionists could save patients from deadly cancers simply by asking whether they would like to schedule a mammogram. Believing in your power to make an impact no matter where you sit is the first step in raising the ceiling on your potential.

STRATEGY #2: DEVELOP YOUR ELEVATED PITCH
(INSTILL THE DESIRE TO LEAD)

In 1998, the Corporation for National and Community Service, the government agency that administers AmeriCorps and other service programs, saw a huge opportunity to expand their impact. They needed to find a way to get youth involved with community volunteering. My sister, Amy Blankson, was in high school at the time and was deeply passionate about the movement. So when she learned about an upcoming leadership conference focusing on this very issue, she tried to sign up. To her surprise, she received a note back saying that the conference was only for adults. Seriously? But instead of feeling disempowered or helpless after being rebuffed, Amy sent a letter to the CNCS board with an impassioned pitch to persuade them that if you want youth to volunteer, you also needed to empower youth to lead. The board was horrified to find out that a youth had been turned away from a conference on youth volunteering and quickly reversed their stance. That year Amy became the very first youth member on the board for the Corporation for National and Community Service. And later that year, at a youth summit in central Texas that she organized, high school students pledged 120,000 volunteer hours for local charities and nonprofits.

In the same way that you don't need to be in an official

leadership role in order to lead, you don't need to be in an official leadership role in order to empower and inspire *others* to do the same. After all, if a passionate high school student can inspire hundreds of other young people to lead change in their communities through volunteering, can't we all expand the power to lead in our own communities and companies?

The key is to **develop an Elevated Pitch**. It's like the typical elevator pitch, only instead of shortening your sales pitch into the time it takes to ride an elevator, an Elevated Pitch is one in which you quickly convince others to be positive forces for change. What is great about the Elevated Pitch is that not only does it motivate people to lead from every seat, but that **the Elevated Pitch can come from any seat**. But convincing people to *want* change is hard no matter where you sit; after all, humans are habitual creatures and can be resistant to ideas that feel new and different. That's why the Elevated Pitch is not something you want to improvise in the moment. It requires time to craft and strategize. When the senior leadership at Kaiser, for example, needed to convince the receptionists to expand their conception of their own potential to see themselves as providers of medical health, it took them weeks to hone their message about how health was interconnected before they were ready to present it to the entire company.

You want to start by thinking of what the recipient of the Elevated Pitch already cares about. For example, if you were trying to inspire a group of sales managers—who you know care about their income and hitting their targets—to embrace a more inclusive style of leadership, you might present them with a study and an example showing how their sales numbers are directly connected to how managers treat their support staff and how much time they spend mentoring junior salespeople on their teams. Or if your goal is to help your extraverted teenager be more motivated in applying to colleges, you might tell her about all the on-campus clubs and activities and opportunities for socializing (that is, parties). The idea is that when you help people see *why* they should want the change, it activates a sense of ownership, turning indifference or inertia into potential.

My mom was a high school English teacher for more than twenty years, and she used to always point out how the lack of ownership in the public school system where she worked was strangling potential. Any time there was a problem or shortfall, rather than take the initiative to do something about it, the administration would blame the state. If the students weren't sustaining gains in their learning, the teachers would blame the parents. And if the students were unhappy? Naturally, they'd blame the teachers. Apathy and blame spread like a virus, and as a result, everyone felt more and more powerless. True leadership is about caring enough to find solutions to problems, instead of continually shifting the blame.

There is no question that failing to encourage engagement and leadership from every seat in companies has a direct impact on business outcomes. In the 2013 Gallup *State of the Global Workplace* report, Gallup found that 63 percent of employees worldwide feel disempowered and disengaged in their jobs, and an additional 24 percent are actively disengaged. According to the report, these employees are not only ineffective, but they often spread their negativity and disengagement to others.[6] The cost of active disengagement in the United States alone is estimated to be more than $500 billion annually—a figure that is hard to ignore.[7] It may be tempting to write off (or lay off) dispirited employees, but in truth this is a short-term,

Band-Aid solution. Long-term organizational success requires that actively disengaged individuals are ushered in a more positive direction, rather than toward the door.

In one Bain & Company study, Michael Mankins and David Harding found a significant quantitative impact of employee engagement on business results. Companies that "attract, deploy, and lead talent more effectively—taking full advantage of the unique skills and capabilities their people bring to the workplace," they wrote, enjoy huge gains in productivity and operating margins that are 30 to 50 percent higher than industry averages.[8] Thanks to their "inspirational leadership and mission-led culture," such companies are able to "unleash far more of their employees' discretionary energy."

A few years ago, I was invited to speak at the insurance giant Allstate. I learned that their CEO was using an Elevated Pitch in an attempt to inspire thirty-five thousand employees—from C-suite executives to initial hires—to buy into the wholesale cultural change he was trying to instill throughout the company. One way to achieve cultural change is to bring in a top-notch outside partner who will perform all of the training—an undertaking that would normally cost millions of dollars. But CEO Tom Wilson knew that forcing people to sit passively in a corporate training session was not the best way to teach ownership. Instead, he wanted to activate an army of champions for positive change. So he and his team set out to create the "Lead from Every Seat" campaign, and invited *employees* to volunteer to lead training sessions for their peers. His Elevated Pitch was that in order to learn leadership skills and rise in the ranks, you must take on the mantle of leadership wherever you are in the company. In the end, 280 volunteer trainers from every level of the company met with Allstate's professional trainers to learn the basics, then were given free rein to put their own unique spin on their presentation.

The result was a mind-blowing display of organic creativity and initiative. Trainers created everything from flash cards to board games to stuffed animals to keep people engaged. Moreover, the fact that the volunteers came from every level of the organization helped break down the barriers of the typical corporate hierarchy; the trainers found it energizing that their boss's boss's boss might actually be sitting in at their training session.

Their enthusiasm was infectious, inspiring their peers to not only complete the training objectives but help keep the momentum of learning and change going. As one volunteer put it, "I am given responsibilities and leadership opportunities on a day-to-day basis that constantly surpass my expectations of what an entry-level position typically looks like. In my first year . . . I was responsible for planning events for thousands of people to raise money for Allstate's domestic violence charity. And now, in my second rotation, I am responsible for interviewing and hiring the next start class of my own program!"[9] That is exactly what we mean when we talk about leading from every seat.[10]

When I spoke at Allstate during their conference to launch and celebrate the initiative, I was impressed by two things. First, by cutting across the different levels of the company's hierarchy, you get an incredible cross-fertilization of ideas and relationships (pillars, bridges, and extenders) to help knit the culture together and speed up expansion of power within the organization. Second, inviting people to lead from every seat had a long-term positive impact. These 280 champions of positive change didn't go back to being just cogs in a wheel, like at other companies; instead, they remained engaged and involved, and constantly raised the ceiling on their leadership potential. Moreover, the fact that their boss's boss's boss might be sitting in at their training session keeps them motivated and on their toes—increasing the chances that they will be promoted, while also opening up more chances for management to discover and promote talent that might have slipped through the cracks.

Similarly, one of the most successful proponents of creating positive organizational change through more inclusive leadership is UnitedHealth Group, particularly the work led by Dave Sparkman, the senior vice president of culture, and his team. Instead of attempting to take on the monumental challenge of changing culture at a company of more than 230,000 employees alone, Dave made an Elevated Pitch inviting people to volunteer to become "culture ambassadors." Given that in order to become a culture ambassador a UnitedHealth employee must go through extra training and take on more responsibility—all without an increase in pay—a cynical person might assume that five to ten people took him up on his offer. But, in fact, the number is much larger. Dave has now deputized ten thousand culture ambassadors at UnitedHealth, and it's growing. People *want* to get involved, not just because they want to learn how to make a better culture but because they want to become better leaders.

When I spoke with Dave at a conference in Phoenix, he had just been to Asia (four times), Brazil, and Europe, all in the last month, making a powerful Elevated Pitch that cultural change requires champions. Little by little, his small but brilliant team of visionaries continues to magnify its impact across the globe, inspiring ambassadors hailing from many countries and speaking many languages to involve themselves in change instead of "waiting on the world to change."

You can use the Elevated Pitch to invite people to be agents of change in your personal life as well. When I was depressed, I told my friends I needed to give them a stake in my mood, and they quickly stepped up to offer me the support I needed. Even parents can encourage their children to take more ownership, perhaps by asking them to take part in family decisions, or giving them a voice in what type of punishment or reward they should receive. Or you can "deputize" them by putting them in charge of watering the herbs you planted together or feeding the pets, or you can give older siblings a role in caring for younger ones.

I remember one night I returned home exhausted from a trip and didn't have the energy to spend an hour fighting my son to get him to sleep. In a moment of inspiration, I asked Leo if *he* would get *me* ready for bed. Excited by his newfound responsibility, he raced through his nightly rituals: all those things I usually needed to do for him, like put his trucks in his bed, put on his PJs, and brush his teeth. Then he covered me with a blanket, kindly gave me one of his trucks to sleep with, and turned off the light, before proudly scurrying back into his own room and promptly falling asleep. Turns out that with a good Elevated Pitch, we can help even a three-year-old activate his leadership potential.

STRATEGY #3: USE PROGRESS AS FUEL (REINFORCE LEADERSHIP)

A division of the $17 billion consulting company Computer Sciences Corporation was facing rough times. According to a case study by Vlatka Hlupic, a professor at Westminster Business School, their growth and profitability had stalled, and thus there was not enough work for their consultants. Revenue was dropping, and yet they still had high costs for salary, which only served to exacerbate the problem.

For all of you who have worked in large companies, you know the typical response. Senior leaders grabbed the reins and started dictating solutions from on high, which unsurprisingly included vicious, morale-killing cuts and layoffs; commands about how to make things more efficient; and demands on employees to work harder for less. Things went from bad to worse when division leaders centralized control, requiring a formal approval process for all consulting projects. As Vlatka wrote, "That caused deterioration of performance, negatively impacted on employee motivation and good employees started to leave as it became harder to replace them. The costs for replacing and training the new employees added to the costs and lowered the operating income. The changes slowed decision-making, reduced risk-taking and eliminated entrepreneurial spirit."[11]

Realizing that this "command and control" model was failing, the division heads decided to take the power out of the sole hands of the top management and EXPAND it throughout the organization. They empowered the consultants to self-organize into teams, which were entrusted to balance the pursuit of performance with the guiding core values of transparency, fairness, and collaboration. Empowered by this newfound decision-making ability and trust, employees at all levels of seniority and experience soon emerged as leaders on the teams. The results were nothing short of astonishing; in year one their profit margin rose 151 percent![12]

But here's the even more amazing part. Simply knowing

exactly how much progress they'd made—down to the percentage point—motivated those leaders to invest more heavily in their teams, making them responsible for ensuring that communication flowed properly and that members of their teams got the resources or mentoring they needed. By year two, profits rose again—this time by 238 percent. Then the power EXPANDed even more. A second division, inspired by these quantified results, tried to replicate the Star System their colleagues had created by granting their own teams more power and autonomy, and their profit margin rose by an even higher 295 percent! Thus, their progress became the fuel of Big Potential.

To sustain change, we must reward and reinforce people's efforts to create change. Thus, it is crucial to use progress to motivate people to continue to lead from every seat. Kaiser Permanente, for example, tracked the success of their program and made sure that the entire staff knew exactly how many lives had been saved. At the Cardinal Community School District, Joel ensured that everyone from crossing guards to lunchroom workers was aware of the tremendous increase in the graduation rate. When people see the fruits of their efforts, it creates a positive feedback loop whereby progress becomes a catalyst for even greater change.

No matter what seat we sit in, we can all use progress to tap into bigger and bigger potential, whether with our teams at work or at home with our kids. If your child is learning to read, for example, you could keep a running list of all the books they have completed to remind them how rewarding reading a book cover to cover can feel. If your team decides to take on a volunteer project, you could bring data or photos to the next meeting reminding them of the impact of their work. Or, if your boss or manager entrusts you with a new project or account, you could show them exactly how your work contributed to bottom-line profits.

Remember that Big Potential is a Virtuous Cycle. The more you expand your power to those around you, the more powerful you become.

STRATEGY #4: LEAD FROM EVERY LUNCH SEAT
(FIND MEANING FROM EVERY SEAT)

One critique I often hear when I talk about "leading from every seat" to individuals and groups comes from people who say, "But what if my job simply doesn't offer a path to leadership, much less a path to Big Potential?" In traveling to more than fifty countries, talking with employees about what motivates them to seek bigger potential, I've also heard many people say that they would be much more engaged, and much more likely to take the initiative to effect change, if they had the perfect job, a supportive boss, the dream position, and so on. I believe, however, that **you can find a path to leadership in almost any job. But first you need a path to meaning.**

The brilliant Amy Wrzesniewski, professor of organizational behavior at Yale University's School of Management, has dedicated much of her research to expanding meaning in our work. According to her research, people view their occupations in one of three ways: as a job, a career, or a calling. A job is merely something to endure in order to get a salary. A career is work that gives you prestige or position within society. A calling is work that you view as integral to your identity and meaning in life, an expression of who you are that gives you a feeling of fulfillment and meaning. A calling is a path to Big Potential.

If asked which jobs in society you would consider to be the *hardest* to see as a calling, rather than a mere job, what would you say? When people are presented with this question on surveys, the common answers are "janitor in a retirement home," "toll booth operator," and "trashman." People generally consider these jobs to rank low in power and low in leadership potential. But Wrzesniewski's research shows that when you ask people whether they view their own work as a job, a career, or a calling, the answers will be fairly consistent across every profession. For example, Wrzesniewski found that executive assistants, hospital employees, and even janitors in retirement homes were equally likely to see their work as a true calling as people in most other professions. In other words, we can all find meaning in our work, no matter what seat we sit in.

To see this in practice, the next time you go to the grocery store, pay attention to the baggers at the end of each checkout row. Most likely what you see will be consistent with the one-third rule that Wrzesniewski describes—a third will look bored and apathetic, a third will look efficient but uninspired, and a third will be cheerful, energetic, and friendly with the customers. Same job, three different responses. I'm guessing that even the happy ones do not want to be grocery baggers the rest of their lives, nor do they think it's the culmination of all their dreams or that it is tapping all their strengths. But they are able to find small ways to create meaning in their jobs nonetheless, whether by making a customer's day brighter with a joke or a compliment, by making the cashier's job easier by finding a way to speed up the line, or doing their part for the environment by encouraging shoppers to use cloth bags instead of plastic.

People like this are proof positive that **not only is leadership a choice; so is meaning.**

But Big Potential starts with you, which means that it's up to you to find that meaning in your current position, so try this now. Are you helping to improve people's lives with your work, even on the smallest scale? Are you able to connect with people at a deeper level? Do you have an opportunity to brighten someone's day because of your interactions? Are you helping improve the world in even a small way? These are not just questions to explore personally, but on teams and in families as well. Research I previously described in *The Happiness Advantage* found that even journaling each day for two minutes about a meaningful experience at work helps your brain not only to identify these moments but also to see ways to infuse more of them into your daily routine.

To dig deeper, ask yourself, Are you able to use your unique skills at work? Your creativity, your emotional intelligence, your knack for numbers? Find a way to make sure you get to use at least one of your unique strengths every day. It is easier to see your work as a calling if you get to bring all of yourself to it.

Many people are unable to see their current work as a calling because they want to do something else someday. As a result, they are so busy romanticizing or obsessing about some future dream job that they forget about all the things that engage them in their current one. Don't get paralyzed by the future. There is nothing wrong with having future goals or ambitions, but if you are constantly looking for greener pastures, you'll never see the beauty of the one you are currently in.

Remember that just as success and potential are not zero-sum games, neither is meaning. **Helping others see the meaning in their personal lives and work lives does not diminish your**

own capacity for meaning; it magnifies it. And that meaning is what empowers us to lead.

Leading from Every Lunch Seat

Africa's first female president was Liberia's famous Ellen Johnson Sirleaf, a hero whose courage allowed her to transcend the labels and expectations placed upon her gender to lead at even the highest levels of government. She wrote, "The size of your dreams must always exceed your current capacity to achieve them. If your dreams do not scare you, they are not big enough." And big dreams require being able to expand our potential beyond what we can accomplish alone. So I'll conclude this chapter with a story reminding us just how much change is possible when we truly dream big.

On day one of college, I met Ann S. Kim. Unlike many of my fellow Harvard students who were pursuing jobs to make the most money, Ann was looking to make the biggest impact. A decade later, Ann was working with the U.S. surgeon general crafting ideas to help create a healthier world. At the cornerstone of Ann's philosophy is her belief that if we want a better world, we have to EXPAND power even to people who seem to have the least of it in our society: children in poverty.

Former surgeon general Vivek Murthy in 2016 said, "I think that if we want to create a healthier country, we need to empower more people to make changes in their lives. But we also have to empower them to help change their environment."[13] Better nutrition is a change that can have a huge impact on the health of our society, particularly for children living in poor environments. So in a partnership with the San Francisco Unified School District and the innovative design firm IDEO, Ann set out looking for ways that a poor elementary school child sitting in a school cafeteria could lead the change toward healthier eating.

It turned out that one of the biggest challenges in getting the students in this district to eat healthier wasn't actually the lack of healthy lunch options in the cafeteria; it was that the kids simply weren't choosing them. The older students hated the lines and the environment of the lunchroom, so the majority of them would abandon the healthy meals in the cafeteria and drive off campus seeking fast food. For the younger kids, the cafeteria experience was fraught with peer pressure and bullying. Kids watched and judged their peers on what came out of their lunch sacks, and as a result some would rather eat nothing, or trade unhealthy options for other unhealthy options, rather than be seen on the lunch line being served food they perceived as far less appealing.

Deconstructing the lunch experience, Ann and her partners at IDEO found that you could short-circuit a lot of these problems by allowing the kids to participate in the lunch experience. Instead of just standing reluctantly in line and waiting for the lunch staff to slop whatever that day's meal happened to be on a plate, the students were assigned rotating roles as "servers," tasked with pushing around carts to take food to their peers. Instead of being individually purchased, food was served family style. A child who had less could simply say, "Please pass the peas" instead of resorting to hunger or bullying. Little by little the students began to feel like they had a voice, which led to them suggesting foods that they'd like. They watched other students select the organic spinach, which encouraged them to also ask for healthy items. The kids were told about the components of their food, and they learned about organics and good fats and gluten, which prompted them to lead as role models for their families when they came home, asking if the cookies were made with healthy oils. The kids became part of the process instead of victims of it.

No lunch plan alone will solve all the problems of health or poverty. But it is a start, and it kicked off a Virtuous Cycle. The administrators saved money because less food was wasted, the school gained pride for the success of such an innovative program, and the community even became safer with fewer teenage drivers speeding out to the nearest fast-food joint. Not to mention that the wholesale improvements in the students' diets led directly to less sickness, higher academic scores, and fewer instances of bullying. And it all started by empowering them to lead from every lunch seat.

When we are brave enough to expand power to others, suddenly we find that a huge weight is lifted off our shoulders, increasing our power to lift even heavier loads. This is the Virtuous Cycle we were seeking. And we can *all* inspire others to dream more, learn more, do more, and become more, no matter what seat we are in.

CHAPTER 5

ENHANCE YOUR RESOURCES

Creating a Prism of Praise and Recognition

Her mentor's words rang in Sarah's ears as she entered the boardroom: "It's either you or her." As Sarah sat down for an afternoon of meetings with partners from her law firm, she knew that in order to be chosen to stand among them as the firm's newest partner, she would need to prove that she was better than the competition.

Getting named to partner was cutthroat, especially that year. There were two extraordinarily good candidates for promotion; only one of them would make partner that round. Both women had been working on the same very large acquisition, and both had made the firm a ton of money.

During the first interview, Sarah had taken her mentor's advice and "sold" herself to one of the partners. She carefully detailed all of her individual accomplishments. She tactfully bragged about her ability to see opportunities where others missed them. Yet she walked out of that meeting feeling like something was off.

Then, during her second interview, this time with a more senior partner, something shifted. When the partner complimented her for her success with the recent acquisition, instead of repeating the same prepared speech from the last session, she replied, "Thank you. That was one of my proudest achievements. But I'm also grateful for the team you surrounded me with on the project. Tim, that new associate you hired, stayed up for three days straight to help me finish. And Karen [the other associate up for partner] worked really hard on the project, too. She is one of the smartest lawyers I've worked with."

She admitted later that she inwardly cringed at the time, fearing that she had just lost the upper hand. Never, ever make the competition look good, right? But, at the same time, acknowledging those colleagues' contributions felt more authentic. So she shared those same sentiments during the rest of her interviews.

A month later she was called into the senior partner's office and told that she got the position. It had been a close race, he told her; in fact, it was just a single difference between the two candidates that clinched the decision. He said that while Karen had used the acquisition as proof that she alone deserved to be partner, Sarah had instead used it to praise the other candidate, the younger associate, and even the partner himself for making good hires. And that, in the end, was what set her apart. The senior partner said, "You made partner because you are not only good, you are good for the firm."

Some people treat praise like a limited commodity. They believe that the key to advancement and success must be to absorb and rack up as much recognition, admiration, and accolades as possible. This is the philosophy we learn in school, then hone to brutal efficiency in the working world. When we mistakenly believe success and recognition are zero-sum, everyone hoards recognition instead of giving it, we become starved for praise, and we eventually become **misers of praise**.

Yet what so many fail to recognize is that **praise is actually a renewable resource**. Praise creates a Virtuous Cycle—the more you give, the more you enhance your own supply. When done right, praise primes the brain for higher performance, which means that the more we praise, the more success we create. And the more successes there are, the more there is to praise.

Instead of praise misers, we need to become Praise Prisms. In physics, a prism is an object with multiple reflective surfaces. When light hits a prism, different wavelengths bend at different angles, creating the rainbow effect when the light reemerges from the prism. In other words, prisms do not merely absorb or deflect light. By shining it on others, they enhance it and make it more beautiful. Sarah was a true Praise Prism: By shining the light of praise outward onto others, rather than absorbing or diminishing it, she not only made her colleagues look good; she also enhanced her own position.

The research I've been doing over the past five years shows that the more you can authentically shine praise on everyone in your ecosystem, the more your potential, both individually and collectively, rises. In *The Happiness Advantage,* I wrote about how when you enhance someone's mood you improve their motivation and performance.[1] In this chapter you'll read new research about how enhancing those around you can improve the *collective* motivation and performance across your ecosystem, thus creating fertile fields for potential to organically grow.

The more praise you give, the more praise you will deserve and then receive. When praise is in abundance, praise misers quickly turn into praise providers; after all, why hoard praise if you do not fear it will be withheld from you? By the same token, the more praise you withhold, the less you get and the less you deserve. Think about it. What would happen if you took all the credit for the success of a group project and the rest of your team found out? At best you'd get a reputation as a poor team player; at worst, your colleagues and boss would be wary of putting you on any future assignments. Or imagine you decided to withhold praise in a romantic relationship. Your partner would probably start withholding not only praise but other things you probably value, which might ultimately make you unhappy in the relationship. As the Persian poet Rumi wrote back in the thirteenth century, "Your depression is connected to your . . . refusal to praise."

I'm not the first to tout the benefits of praise. And I'm willing to guess that most people reading this book recognize that praise is invaluable, whether as leaders or as parents. But the problem in most of our businesses, schools, and relationships isn't just that we fail to praise enough; it's that we have been praising the wrong way. I would go so far as to say that our current model of praise demotivates the vast majority of our teams, exacerbates internal strife in our families, and places a cap on our potential.

At the core of the problem is how we handle praise and recognition in our own lives. Our response to praise is often to either deflect it, whether out of shyness or humility (for example, "I just got lucky"), or absorb it, out of the misguided belief that it is in short supply. In both cases, the praise is stifled and the light is extinguished before it can have a chance to fully shine.

We must find a way to take in the light of praise and refract that light outward.

By denying the light of praise, we extinguish it. By bending the light toward others, we magnify it.

If we want to truly engage, motivate, and inspire, whether as leaders or parents, we need to completely *rethink* praise. There are a few specific mistakes we make that cause us to inadvertently snuff out the light of praise, and it's not just that we are praising the outcomes instead of the process, as Stanford professor Carol Dweck wrote about in the excellent book *Mindset*. For one, our instinct is often to point out things that people are doing wrong, even when our intention is to highlight what they are doing right. Second, we tend to praise people by comparing them to others; that is, lifting one person up at the expense of another. We overemphasize praising the top performers (who usually already have their reward) instead of the collective efforts of the team, and we expect praise to trickle from the top down instead of flowing freely in all directions.

In this chapter you'll learn six strategies for magnifying the power of praise, whether in your company, community, or family:

STRATEGY #1: Stop comparison praise.

STRATEGY #2: Spotlight the right.

STRATEGY #3: Praise the base.

STRATEGY #4: Democratize praise.

STRATEGY #5: Unlock the Hidden 31.

STRATEGY #6: Don't just praise the outcome; praise *to* an outcome.

STRATEGY #1: STOP COMPARISON PRAISE

The worst piece of praise I've sometimes received after a talk is "You were the best speaker today." What's so bad about that? you ask. Well, first of all, it undercuts all the other speakers. What if another speaker was standing next to me? Moreover, it reminds me of the fact that in many cases I *won't* be the best speaker, so now I feel nervous and self-conscious. Instead of enhancing me, this comment unbalances me in the future.

This is an example of one of the most common mistakes I see people make with praise: giving such compliments as "Your report was better than Jack's" or "You're the smartest person in the room" or "You were the best player out there on the field." Why? **Because what you are actually doing is comparing, not praising.** You are attempting to prop people up by kicking others down! Real praise is telling someone "Your report was amazing," or "The comedic timing of your speech was perfect," not telling them that their report or their speech was better than another person's.

When you tell someone that they are "better" than someone else, that by definition means that someone else is "worse." Moreover, by telling someone they are "better" or "the best," you are placing an unconscious, implicit limit on your expectation for what that other person can achieve. Also, if we are striving only to be better than someone else, doesn't that set our expectations for ourselves too low? It tells us that as soon as we are just a little bit better than another person, we can stop trying, even if it means stopping short of our potential.

If you want to enhance others, do not compare them. In truth, this was the hardest lesson of the book for me to write, because I thought I was intuitively praising others, including my wife and son. But I now know I was making a crucial mistake. No matter how good your intentions, if you excitedly say to a child "You were the best one out there!" you just taught them that your love and excitement were predicated on their position compared to others. Nothing undercuts Big Potential more than comparison praise. But it is so easy to inadvertently do.

Think how often we fall for the comparison trap. "You are the hottest/smartest/funniest person in this room." Why do we have to diminish everyone else in the room in an attempt to praise one individual? And what if that individual were to move to another room filled with more attractive/smarter/funnier people? Why not simply say, "You are beautiful and smart and funny"? Comparison praise feeds into the Small Potential mentality that success—or leadership, creativity, beauty, love, or anything else that we care about—are limited resources; it exacerbates the Small Potential zero-sum mentality of success. When you tell a group of people that only a certain percentage of them can be successful, you are dampening everyone's drive, ambition, and potential.

The easiest way to stop comparison praise is simply to eliminate superlatives from our vocabulary—"the best," "the fastest," "the smartest," "the prettiest." All of these undercut others instead of telling people they are great in their own right. Instead, follow what I consider an inviolable law of praise for leaders and parents: **Do not compliment at the expense of others.**

What's the best compliment I could get after my talk? It's not about my speaking style; it's when someone tells me they are going to start doing one of the positive habits I spoke about, or they're going to buy my book for a friend who is struggling. The most authentic way to acknowledge someone is to change your behavior. **The best praise is by actions changed.**

Our culture, and particularly our school systems, are rife with a subtle but dangerous form of comparison praise. Each year in most of our top universities, a sizable number of well-despised professors take an ill-advised philosophical stand against grade inflation by creating a strict grading curve for their classes. The concept of the grading curve is based on the mistaken belief that if you impose performance ratings, it will improve performance. But in truth it does anything but.

First of all, in dictating that only a small number of students can get A's, we are essentially communicating to students that academic achievement is a limited resource: exactly the opposite of what we are trying to achieve with Big Potential. Second, these are students who were at the tops of their classes in their schools back home, so why would we automatically assume that 30 percent of them would be C students in college? And finally, this system discourages students—the same ones who may really have liked to learn the content being taught—from taking the classes out of fear of lowering their grade point averages.

Some would argue that such competition is healthy. Or that forcing a false curve on top-performing students is necessary to weed out all but the cream-of-the-crop performers for things like pre-med classes. But given that we live in a society with a huge shortage of doctors, this rationale doesn't hold water; in fact, the "weed-out" is mostly because colleges don't have enough pre-med professors. And even if that were not the case, why would you weed out people in their first year in college while they are still learning the ropes—when many of them may have made excellent doctors, were they given the chance to learn? We are snuffing out potential before even giving it room to grow. And instead of getting an elite group of superstar doctors, you get stressed-out, maybe even drugged-out, students and not enough doctors to treat them. They become like the hyper-competitive chickens from chapter 2; instead of becoming super producers, everyone ends up pecking each other to death.

In the working world, we suffer the pox of comparison praise in the form of performance reviews, particularly those that "grade" employees on some numerical scale. This may sound harmless enough in theory, but these types of assessments end up having the same effect in practice as the grading curve; when managers mistakenly believe that only a finite number of their employees can be "A" performers, they end up demotivating and stirring up resentment among all those who end up with lower grades.

In one fascinating article published in the *Harvard Business Review*, David Rock from the NeuroLeadership Institute posited a few more reasons why performance reviews should be obsolete, arguing that the numerical rating systems used by many companies don't take into account how work gets done today. Work is happening in teams more than ever, he argues, with many people working on multiple teams that are often spread throughout the world. "Few managers accurately know their team members' performance when that employee is involved in many other teams, often doing work the manager doesn't see or even understand," he writes. "Standard performance reviews, delivered once a year, are just not relevant to the ways we work anymore."[2]

But would people get less praise and less constructive feedback if we were to eliminate performance reviews? Actually, the opposite is true. Of the thirty top companies studied by the NeuroLeadership Institute, managers were actually giving constructive feedback and praise three to four times more often in the *absence* of performance reviews. Luckily, some innovative companies are embracing this idea more readily. Over the years, I've spent quite a bit of time working with Adobe in Northern California. Back in 2011, management called a town hall meeting to discuss what they had found to be the biggest stumbling block to engagement scores and happiness: the one-to-five performance rating system for the employees. They did away with the system completely once they recognized the negative impact it was having on attracting and keeping good talent. Even GE, which famously pioneered the idea of ranking employees and then eliminating the bottom 10 percent, has largely done away with this outdated system.

Theodore Roosevelt once said, "Comparison is the thief of joy." If we really want to enhance others, we must stop comparing.

STRATEGY #2: SPOTLIGHT THE RIGHT

At the end of 2016, I signed a deal with Princess Cruise Lines; they wanted me to come aboard and research how engagement, positivity, and happiness among their staff impacted the guest experience. And clearly the only way to do that was to go on a cruise. The week of the cruise happened to fall on the week of my mom's seventieth birthday and my parents' fortieth wedding anniversary. So that's how it happened that I ended up bringing twenty-six people with me on my "business trip."

Ever supportive of my work, my family members soon set sail on their own missions to "research" happiness. Some explored happiness through the artisan chocolates and all-you-can-eat deliciousness. Some of the more ambitious ones were intent on learning how happiness would vary depending upon which country we were docked in. My then-two-year-old son, for example, concluded (based on his rigorous three hours of research each day before his nap) that Belize was the best because it definitely had "more trucks." While he was busy researching trucks per capita, I was meeting with the crew to better understand the factors that contributed to their levels of engagement, and in turn how well they engaged and served the vacationing passengers.

On the second day of the cruise, the head of my research team, my sister, and I ventured down into the bowels of the ship to tour the crew's rooms, mess hall, and facilities. Then we sat down to interview thirty crew members about their experiences working on the ship. With each interview I would ask: "Please think about the best days you have had while working on this contract. What was it that made it such a good day?"

I expected that most would tell me their best days had been when they got shore leave to go explore the rain forests, or when they scored a free afternoon to spend lounging on the pool deck, or perhaps when they got to spend an evening partying with their fellow crew members. But much to my surprise, one after another, they told me that the best days were the ones in which they received a kind word of praise from their direct supervisor. My sister and I looked at each other skeptically, then pushed for more answers. **But by the time the eighth or ninth crew member told us that praise from a direct manager was the best part of their experience, we realized that we had stumbled upon something significant.**

Think about this for a second. This crew, made up of mostly young people in their twenties, are literally on a floating pleasure ship, seeing the world and visiting exotic destinations. And yet, the times they felt most positive and motivated were not when they got to go off exploring or partying, but instead when they received a comment from their leader spotlighting what they were doing well.

But here comes the most important part. We found that when they were feeling enhanced by the recognition of a manager, they were also more likely to refract this positive energy onto the guests, through friendlier and more helpful interactions, greater efficiency and quality of service, and consistently going the extra mile to make their vacations that much better. We soon realized that one of the most powerful ways to enhance a guest experience was to ensure that managers were authentically and frequently spotlighting what their staff was doing right.

The nineteenth-century poet and playwright Oscar Wilde wrote, "When men give up *saying* what is charming, they give up *thinking* what is charming" (italics mine). This is a perfect way of describing the neuroscience behind "Spotlight the right," a strategy Michelle and I used in our PBS program *Inspire Happiness*. What we say and do tells our brain what to focus on. So if you aren't actively scanning the social ecosystem for things to praise, your brain fails to notice what's going on right. By the same token, what we focus on tells our brain what to repeat. As Oprah said in my interview for *Super Soul Sunday*, "The more you praise and celebrate your life, the more there is in life to celebrate."

In the same way that praise focuses the brain on positive behavior, criticism focuses the brain on negative behavior. And since what we focus on is what gets repeated, why would we want to spotlight what's wrong instead of what's right? This is exactly why most performance reviews actually lower performance. Too many managers highlight the points of weakness or areas for improvement first, before highlighting the positive. From the perspective of the brain, this tells the employee that the manager cares not about their strengths but their weaknesses; not their growth but their deficits. Thus the brain believes that their positive behaviors do not matter. And what does not matter does not get repeated.

This is not to say that managers should not give honest feedback, or point out areas for improvement and growth. We have to be realistic about the weaknesses or challenges we need to overcome. But we must also recognize that to improve our shortfalls and weaknesses, rather than ignore them, requires mental resources, strength, and energy. Praise is what provides access to those resources. It fuels us as we work to improve and grow.

Some managers believe that neutral feedback—feedback containing neither explicit criticism nor explicit praise—is better than overtly critical feedback, but in fact that's not the case. Not only is failing to give praise a wasted opportunity to reinforce positive behaviors; in the absence of praise, our brain goes straight to the negative, causing us to *perceive* criticism of our work. Brent Furl, one of today's most enterprising young neuroscientists, explains that when we perceive criticism, rejection, or fear, "our bodies produce higher levels of neurochemicals that shut down the thinking center of our brains and activates protection behaviors. We become more reactive and sensitive. We often perceive even greater judgment and negativity than actually exists."

Remember, attention tells the brain what to repeat. Thus, if we want to encourage excellence, we need a daily practice to shine attention on instances of excellence. The most powerful one in my life, and one that I suggest in every talk, is to take two minutes (maximum) each morning to simply write and send a text message or email praising or thanking someone in your life. Of all the positive habits I have, this is the most powerful one for multiple reasons. First, you have just scanned your relationships for something positive to spotlight, helping you see more positives, which, in turn, gives you more to spotlight. When I suggest this at companies, managers say that that simple email in the morning causes them to look for and see more things to praise and recognize on their teams the rest of the day.

So stop reading for a moment and try this experiment out. Send a text to someone in the favorites list of your phone contacts, praising or thanking them for something authentic. Going forward, try to pick a new person every day—a friend, a coworker, an old coach, your kid's teacher, your aunt, your doctor. The more you praise, the more it becomes second nature.

Not only does spotlighting the right encourage positive behavior; it makes people feel good—which, in turn, makes you feel good as well. Better yet, you'll find that people will generally reflect praise back on you; you'll be surprised by how many amazing notes you get back over the course of your day telling you how great you are! You have just enhanced their world, and as a result they enhance yours. And you've given them license to praise, turning them into praise providers and igniting a Virtuous Cycle.

Whether we run a cruise ship, a company, a classroom, or anything else, if we want to help others raise their performance and potential, we need to help them focus their attention on what they are doing right. Like light bending and refracting when coming in contact with a prism, when we deliver praise correctly, that praise is reflected right back in our direction, only magnified. But in order to do so, we need to learn to bend the light to shine attention on the base.

STRATEGY #3: PRAISE THE BASE

Over the past decade, I have attended and spoken at more than five hundred sales conferences. That's right: five hundred. By now, I have seen everything. At my very first one, I walked awkwardly onto the stage and was immediately engulfed by a hazy cloud created by fog machines pointed directly at me while "Welcome to the Jungle" blared in the background at full volume . . . after which I gave a talk on mindfulness research and how to "cancel the noise" in our lives (seriously). At another conference, the leader who introduced me took a sledgehammer to a "glass" wall that had been erected onstage (it was actually a pane of clear sugar) to demonstrate how pumped and ready they were to "break down all the sales barriers." After the first two hammer blows didn't work, the third strike shattered the wall, eliciting screams as sugar shrapnel flew into the front rows of attendees—who of course assumed it was glass flying at their faces. Another time, I followed a longhorn steer onstage. I'm not sure why. The point is, while these sales conferences seem to be full of new surprises, after five hundred talks, I have learned there is also a constant.

At some point in the conference, you can reliably predict that you will be able to sit back and listen to some senior leaders, or maybe even the CEO, do exactly what they were taught to do in business school: praise. Weeks earlier, they had their assistants find out who had earned the most revenue, or closed the most deals, or brought in the most business. Now they invite those winners onstage. They list their achievements and successes. They shake hands with them and take a picture. Then they send them back to their VIP seats. Meanwhile, the other 95 percent of employees are sitting in the audience, usually texting or checking ESPN.com on their phones, feeling, at best, bored or apathetic; at worst, full of despair or disdain.

This type of praise—recognition that goes only to the highest performer—is Small Potential praise. Small Potential praise shines on one person already at the top, then flames out there. **Big Potential praise shines on the support system that made high performance possible.** That support system, whether it's coworkers or family or friends, is your "base"—and when you praise that base, you lift up the entire system that rests upon it.

I know some readers might be thinking that I'm advocating giving everyone on the losing team trophies. I'm not. Giving out trophies to everyone is inauthentic, and the research is clear that if you give people inauthentic praise, it backfires by eliminating trust.[3] Instead, I'm saying that when we praise a win, we need to also recognize the supporting players who make the wins possible. I am *not saying to stop* praising the high performers, or to praise only the low performers. I'm saying that we need to redirect *more* light to the player who made the assist, not just the player who scored the winning goal, because the latter already received their due with the adulation of the crowd and the thrill of the goal. In most companies, the high performers have already received their rewards in terms of higher grades, higher pay, or a higher title. So we need to make sure we are also rewarding the people who make less visible, yet no less valuable, contributions to the team's success. Keep the light on the base steady and it will reflect upward and outward, so that the top shines even brighter.

We often spend so much time and energy focusing on enhancing high-performing individuals that we ignore the *collective morale of the team*. In their journal article "Feeling Good Makes Us Stronger: How Team Resilience Mediates the Effect of Positive Emotions on Team Performance," researchers from Spain expanded upon Barbara Fredrickson's research on individual emotions and looked instead at the collective emotional state of the team.[4] What they found was that even in the presence of one or two positive people, if the team collectively is not resilient, both the results of the team as a whole *and the individual* performance of the people on it drop. Because rewarding only the top performers inevitably breeds jealousy, envy, and unhealthy competition, it is the quickest way to shatter a team's resilience, morale, and trust.

Nick Saban, the head coach of the University of Alabama football team and one of the most successful coaches ever, does not practice praise like most coaches do. Saban doesn't typically gush about individual players. He doesn't give out game balls to the MVP. Singling out anyone like that, he explains, would go against the goal of lifting up the entire team. He knows that no football player wins the championship alone, just as no high performer at anything achieves success alone. He believes that **collective wins should get collective praise**.

Former Missouri coach Gary Pinkel says about Saban, "It's crazy what he's done, almost miraculous. He gets the best players, but he gets those players to buy into his system and buy into the team. That's the key. They're playing for each other, not for themselves or for anybody else, and I think that's a big reason they're always playing so well in these [playoff] kinds of games."[5] By praising the base he manages to enhance the entire Star System, not just a single superstar.

The military, too, knows how to do praise well. When I was at boot camp for my Navy ROTC scholarship, they didn't single out the fastest runners or the best marchers. After all, in a combat situation, it doesn't matter how fast any one individual can run; if one man in your platoon lags behind, you're all in trouble. So in ROTC, if one person can't get over the wall, everyone has to start over. If the entire team doesn't make it to the designated point at the specified time, everyone runs. If one person falls off the inflatable boat, you flip the boat so everybody falls. *We succeed together or fail alone.* This philosophy is at the heart of Big Potential, and it's one we desperately need to adopt in our schools and companies.

It is myopic for anyone to think their achievement, no matter how big or small, happened in a vacuum. This is why, whenever I receive praise—perhaps I receive an email from someone saying how much one of my books changed their life, or I get a standing ovation after a talk—I always tell my team, "We got a great email." Or "We got asked to speak at a big conference." Because we did; though my name might have been the one on the cover of the book, and though I may have been the one standing on the stage, my team's efforts are a part of every book I write and every speech I give. The same is true for you. That's not humility, that's reality.

So whenever you receive praise, first ask yourself who helped get you to that place. You're not looking to minimize your accomplishment; you want to refract the recognition, rather than absorb it or deflect it. You want to highlight those who helped you get there, whether it's the research staff who compiled the data you used to close the deal, the running back who took the ball up the field, or the family member who quizzed you on the night before exams. In doing so you ENHANCE the very system that continually earns you more praise—your base.

By the same token, when you practice praising someone via email or text each morning, try to ask yourself who else contributed to that person's success. For example, if you send a message to your colleague congratulating him on the outstanding results of his clever marketing campaign, send a similar note to the assistant who helped him execute it. Michael Jordan said, "Talent wins games, but teamwork and intelligence wins championships." Our praise should flow to the support players, not just the superstars.

Instead of bringing only the top performers up to the stage, we need to invite those who helped support their success, whether it is an assistant, a worker in the warehouse, a mentor, or someone else. And when we do invite the top performers, we should have them thank their top supporter onstage. Instead of lavishing more attention on the superstars already in the spotlight, it redirects a light on the rest of the stars who don't always get the opportunity to shine.

And in our schools and families, we must realize that when one kid does well, we have an incredible opportunity to lift up the support that got them there. For example, we can offer a thank-you to the younger brother who sat in the cold to cheer his brother on when he scored the goal. Or we can show how much we appreciate the older sister who helped teach her younger one to read. When our kids excel in a subject or topic in school, we could encourage them to thank their teachers for the role they played in that success.

When it comes to praising the base, specificity and authenticity are key. What that means is you shouldn't tell the junior employee "Thanks for helping on that project"; you should tell them exactly how their work directly contributed to the project's success. You shouldn't just thank your middle son for being a "supportive sibling"; you should point out the ways in which he made his brother feel supported. The more specific you are, the more authentic the praise will feel and the more likely people will be to bounce it back to others.

In the modern world, individual achievements have become passé. No single person makes computer chips with faster processing speeds, no single person invents a new drug, and no single person cures cancer. Going forward, the best discoveries and advances will be made by Star Systems, not individual superstars. We'd do well to keep this in mind when we dole out recognition and praise.

STRATEGY #4: DEMOCRATIZE PRAISE

In a *Harvard Business Review* article, I once described an interaction with a leader at a Fortune 100 company who told me, "We don't need a praise and recognition program. We pay people to be engaged." This is a surprisingly common refrain from unenlightened leaders—an assumption based upon the belief that high pay equals high engagement. Ironically, I would argue that actually HE was paid to get people engaged, which means that if he wasn't praising, he wasn't doing his job.

A good leader praises the people who make success possible. A *great* leader does not merely praise other people, but, rather, turns other people into praise providers themselves.

At a time when so many people are feeling overworked and

underappreciated in their jobs and workplace, how can you transform passivity into praise? Remember that with a prism, multiple surfaces are needed to bend and refract the light. The same must be true for praise in our organizations, schools, and workplaces. We must activate a culture in which everyone, regardless of what seat they sit in, can participate in shining the light of praise, instead of waiting for it to come from the top down. In other words, we need to democratize praise. Think of this as a marriage of two paths to Big Potential: We must EX-PAND our power to ENHANCE others. We need to turn people into praise providers, not praise misers.

Two new research studies that I've been a part of are paving the way to a number of novel Internet-era solutions for democratizing praise. The idea for this research germinated when I spoke at the WorkHuman conference in 2015 alongside Adam Grant, Arianna Huffington, and Rob Lowe, who despite being experts in different fields had a consistent message: We need to find effective, scalable solutions to create a positive and engaged workforce.

Specifically, I wanted to find out how we could use technology to operationalize praise and recognition in a way that would positively impact business outcomes. I began by partnering with Globoforce, creators of a tool that allows employees across a company to publically share recognition, compliments, and acknowledgment of their colleagues through a company-wide social feed that allows every person in the organization to see and emulate one another's successes in real time. The fruits of that labor are starting to materialize and could help provide a model for shaping better recognition programs at work.

We began by testing this tool with JetBlue Airways. After being recognized by J.D. Power as the highest in customer satisfaction among low-cost carriers for eleven years running, JetBlue had recently suffered a drop in employee engagement as it struggled to scale its positive and service-driven culture following a period of explosive growth. The company was looking to get back to some of its core values of teamwork, caring, and culture, and recognized that to do so it needed to put praise front and center.

So Globoforce built JetBlue a social "peer-to-peer" recognition program whereby any "crew member" (as employees are called) could nominate a coworker to be acknowledged for exemplary effort or performance. That acknowledgment would then be shared throughout the company on an internal newsfeed, where coworkers could publically post their own notes of thanks or congratulations. The recipient of the recognition would also be given "points," much like credit card points or frequent-flier miles, that they could spend as they wished. They could elect to redeem the reward immediately for a gift card to a popular restaurant, for example, or they could opt to save up for a bigger-ticket item, such as a vacation or a cruise. The idea was to democratize praise across the organization so that anyone, no matter their role or rank in the company, could both enhance, and be enhanced by, any of their peers.

The results were impressive, leading to significantly higher levels of employee performance and engagement, as well as increased customer loyalty. Specifically, **for every 10 percent increase in instances of recognition, JetBlue saw a 3 percent increase in retention and a 2 percent increase in engagement**, and an external evaluation by Symantec found a 14 percent increase in engagement scores overall. Given that turnover can be one of the most expensive problems at a company (the costs of replacing an employee range from 20 to 150 percent of their salary), a 3 percent change in retention can represent tens of millions of dollars, depending on the scale of the company. In addition, the JetBlue data showed that engaged crew members were three times more likely to "wow" their customers and twice as likely to be disproportionately singled out in positive feedback reported by customers. Thus, democratizing recognition is not just an issue of keeping employees happy; it has an impact upon customer satisfaction and loyalty as well.

A digital system for giving praise isn't cold and impersonal; it is merely a platform that empowers more people to be Prisms of Praise. Not only does it allow us to enhance people on a larger scale, but because the recognition is completely voluntary—not mandated by an HR initiative or performance review—it feels more like an organic expression of gratitude, which is exactly what it is. And because each recipient gets to choose what is meaningful to *them* as a reward, they end up with something much more personal than, say, some generic, mass-produced plaque, while also avoiding awkward incidents such as a vegan getting a free steak dinner, or a deaf employee receiving an iPod (both true stories of recognition gone wrong). And finally, the shared nature of the recognition enhances not only the recipient but also all those in the company who see accomplishments being appreciated and recognized and are motivated and inspired by them. As the Roman poet Cicero said, "Gratitude is not only the greatest of virtues, but the parent of all the others."

Let me be clear: I'm not suggesting that recognition be in lieu of deserved pay increases; they can and should work in tandem. I'd love it if every company could give raises to the average worker for doing great work. But as companies do not have unlimited funds and many will inevitably fall on hard times, it's unquestionably better to reward people with appreciation and respect than with nothing at all. And because research shows that praise enhances not only a company's employee satisfaction but also its bottom line, it can contribute to a more robust financial picture that supports increases in pay.

In fact, a research project I did with LinkedIn in partnership with Christina Hall, Jimmy Nguyen, and Libby Brendin revealed that the ROI on praise may be even higher than we realize. Incredibly, we found that the dollar amount attached to an award had little bearing upon engagement and turnover rates. But the *frequency* of praise did. If someone received just three or more touchpoints, or instances, of praise in a single quarter, their performance score in the next review period significantly increased. **If they received four or more touchpoints of praise or recognition in a quarter, the retention rate increased to 96 percent over the next year.** New hires have an 80 percent retention rate, but if they get one touchpoint of praise, nothing happens. If they get two, the retention rate stays about the same. At three or four touchpoints of praise, the retention rate is 94 percent. That's stunning. Given that the cost of replacing an average employee could be around $40,000, if we do the math we see that every single short touchpoint of praise was worth $10,000! This is a crucial reminder to us at work and at home. It's not single moments of praise that count, but rather our ability to magnify the total praise in our lives.

But here is the finding that I find most amazing: If the individual received four or more touchpoints of praise over the year, the amount of praise that they *provided to their peers* doubled. We found a magical tipping point: **Those who were praised become praise providers at four or more touchpoints of praise.** Thus, you have created a Virtuous Cycle by which praise continuously multiplies. You may even have tapped into a crucial resource for enhancing your own power to enhance others: the Hidden 31.

STRATEGY #5: UNLOCK THE HIDDEN 31

Remember that if we want to create a Virtuous Cycle of praise, we need to find a way to turn other people into praise providers. For that, we need to activate a special sleeper cell of fundamentally positive people. In a cross-industry research study I did with my wife and fellow positive psychology researcher Michelle Gielan in partnership with *Training* magazine, we found that a whopping 31 percent of people report being "positive but not expressive of it at work." In positive systems research we call these people "the Hidden 31," and we consider them to be the key to creating greater ripple effects of praise. These people are one step short of being champions of positivity at work. They are already optimistic; you just need to enhance them.

Since publishing this work, Michelle and I are often asked whether positive people or negative people have more power to influence the overall tenor of an ecosystem. The research answer is neither. The people who have the most power are the ones who are the most *expressive* of their mindset, positive or negative. The problem is that most systems have this huge class of people—31 percent—who are engaged and positive but are not expressing it, which means that the social script is largely being written by the more vocal negative individuals. The key, then, is to find a way to bring this Hidden 31 out of the shadows and into the light.

Of course, before you turn the Hidden 31 into an army of praise providers, you have to figure out who they are in the first place. You can do this in a number of ways, from formal surveys to informal conversations. For example, in one study, we simply asked people, "On a scale of one to five, how expressive are you of your optimism at work?" Or you can ask, "On a scale of one to five, how comfortable do you feel complimenting the work of someone on your team?" Or "When you are feeling optimistic, how receptive do you find your manager?" When people report being optimistic but not expressive of it, those are your low-hanging fruit for change. Too often, well-meaning managers focus on converting the most pessimistic person in the room. Instead of going guns blazing after the biggest detractors, activating these closet optimists can transform a culture from negative or neutral to net positive.

I don't think it's biased or an exaggeration to say that my wife, Michelle's, book is one of the two most important books written in the last two thousand years. (Yeah, I realize I just engaged in comparison praise.) I'm a proud husband, and in *Broadcasting Happiness* she describes two excellent strategies for activating the Hidden 31. First, you boost your own "signal" by providing more praise. As you are more expressive in praising others (whether verbally, or even just by smiling encouragingly at someone during a conversation), you are essentially modeling how to express praise, while also shifting the tone of the conversation to a more positive one. (Just make sure you're being a rational optimist, not someone who is out of touch with reality.) Second, after identifying the Hidden 31, suggest ways they can test out being expressive without a high cost, maybe by encouraging them to send a congratulatory email or priming them to chime in during a conversation where you are acknowledging someone for strong performance. (For example, "Bob's presentation was terrific, wasn't it?") This way, even the introverts can find safe ways to express their positivity.

I think this research is important, because the best way to get someone to express what they are thinking or feeling is to let them know that they are not alone. If you are a positive person but feel like the people around you are not positive, you can take heart: Thirty-one percent of the people around you at work who may not currently seem particularly engaged or positive actually ARE, they just aren't showing it. Which means you have a one-in-three chance that the seemingly neutral or negative person you are talking to is actually an optimist. And once you show that *you* feel safe expressing praise and positivity, you'd be surprised how many people open up.

STRATEGY #6: DON'T JUST PRAISE THE OUTCOME; PRAISE *TO* AN OUTCOME

Every year, the day before the start of classes at Harvard, nervous and excited freshmen gather at the annual activity fair, where they wander around checking out the various booths and daydreaming about all the fun clubs they're going to join, the exclusive societies they're going to pledge, and the championship-winning athletic teams they're going to try out for. And every year, Coach Blocker stands in front of Sever Hall, yards away from where the fair is held, and he scans the freshmen. Among the alumni it is well-known that he does this every year. However, among the freshmen, it is not. I was no exception. All I knew was when I walked past Sever Hall that afternoon a large man with ruddy cheeks suddenly appeared in my path, extended his meaty fist at me, pointed, and said, "Son, have you ever rowed crew? You have the ideal body to be incredibly successful at the sport."

Now, you might think that I would have been skeptical of such a compliment. I weighed maybe a buck fifty soaking wet, and I think most birds would have questioned whether my twig legs could support their weight. But instead of considering whether perhaps this man had a rare vision disorder, I felt like the Oracle had parted the masses and pointed me out as The One. I responded that I had never rowed before, which was putting it lightly. (In reality I had never been *in* a boat before, unless you count a houseboat on Lake Waco.) Coach Blocker then put his meaty fist on my shoulder and confided, "Well then, son, I'll teach you personally. You need to be at my special invite-only meeting tonight at the Boathouse at eight P.M. as I create my team for freshman crew."

I couldn't even wait until the activity fair was over before calling my parents to proudly announce that I was being recruited to the freshman crew team. Which makes the next part of the story that much more embarrassing. When I arrived at eight P.M., I found myself in a room full of more than a hundred freshmen, all there to row freshman crew. The meeting was invite only, true. But what Blocker had failed to mention was that he had invited basically the entire freshman class. And as it turns out, he had done so not just this once, but year after year.

At a time when impressionable young freshmen were starving for attention and direction, he singled them out for praise. And suddenly one hundred students who may or may not have had the right body type for crew found themselves at the introductory meeting picking "starboard or portside"—even though most couldn't tell the difference. Of course, many won't make it through the first practice, and many more won't last a full season. But the point is that Blocker gave them an *opportunity to try*. Sometimes he finds a diamond in the rough—a student who rows freshman crew and ends up making the world-famous varsity team. And even when he doesn't, his praise, while indiscriminate and far-flung, helps students *believe* in their own potential, thus lifting the ceiling on what they can achieve.

(In case you're wondering, I made it to the spring before my boat got stuck under a mooring and six of the eight of us swallowed too much dirty Charles River water to keep competing. But I'm proud that I rowed crew.)

When we attempt to enhance others, we are all too often focused on *past* successes or outcomes. But praise can be fuel for future ones, as well, because it helps us believe in our potential going forward. In other words, we need to praise not only past achievements and efforts, but also the ones we want to strive for in the future.

One way to do this is to take a page from Coach Blocker's playbook and ascribe people qualities that predict some future potential. For example, "You'd be such a great leader here because you care so much about the company." Or "You'd make such a great asset to the crew team because you look so strong and athletic." My story aside, this type of praise works far better when it's authentic, but what generally happens is that people attach "love for the company" or "athletic physique" to their self-identity, which then reinforces the very trait that will help them become a better leader, earn a spot on the crew team, and so on.

Those who have seen me give a talk have probably heard me quip that people are "familiar with my hometown, Waco, but for the wrong reasons." (I used to assume that many people connect it with the David Koresh cult from the 1990s or the 2015 biker gang brawl.) But today, HGTV's wildly popular reality show *Fixer Upper* has put Waco back on the map, and thankfully with a positive narrative. For the uninitiated, the show follows a couple named Chip and Joanna as they go around Waco transforming dilapidated, run-down homes into beautiful places for families to live. When Chip was asked what it is that excites him about fixing up homes, he said, "I just like to take things that others deem unworthy and make them worthy."

I love this life philosophy, because it acknowledges the beauty of future potential. By enhancing others and helping them to see their worth, we can turn them into prisms of light that enhance everyone around them. That kind of power is Big Potential in action.

A week later Leo and I were at Target "visiting our friends" in the toy aisle (that means we hang out for a while but we don't bring any of them home), when suddenly I spotted some plush characters from *Inside Out*. I excitedly yelled out, "Look, Leo, JOY!" His eyes opened wide, a huge smile came on his face, and with ecstatic glee, he reached for the stuffed creature next to Joy and yelled, "SADNESS!" *Oh no you didn't,* I thought. I again enthusiastically pointed out Joy, while he contentedly disregarded me and snuggled in close to Sadness. Realizing the preciousness of the moment, I grabbed another Sadness off the shelf, and for five minutes a happiness researcher sat cross-legged on a floor in Target cradling Sadness with his son.

This simple moment parallels one of the most important and deepest lessons of this book: Contrary to what many people believe, emotions like sadness, fear, and anger do not obstruct the path to Big Potential. To the contrary: They are necessary and useful. I say in my talks that the opposite of happiness is not unhappiness. Unhappiness can, in fact, fuel incredible positive change: Unhappiness reminds me when I'm lonely and need to reach out to my friends, unhappiness tells me when I'm doing something that goes against my core values, and unhappiness tells me when my work is not in line with my priorities. The opposite of joy is not sadness; it is apathy, which is the loss of energy to continue to pursue one's goals. If you lose your joy, the pursuit of Big Potential becomes both meaningless and futile.

We long for life to be perfect, both at work and at home. Surely we could experience more joy and achieve more success in a world where everything goes our way, everyone agrees with us, and work is always fun. And we get frustrated when these things do not occur. The biggest stumbling block for some readers of this book will be trusting in our ability to achieve Big Potential when the world seems to be rewarding the wrong things and even punishing the good ones. John Mayer expresses the frustration in song with the lyrics "Now we see everything that's going wrong / With the world and those who lead it / . . . So we just keep on waiting (waiting) / Waiting on the world to change."

But if we keep waiting, the world will never change. **We may not have the power to control the world, but we do have the power to DEFEND the good within it.**

The good news is we can give up waiting for a perfect world to support us in our pursuit of Big Potential. We do not need to despair if we experience fear, anger, or sadness. In fact, they are crucial. They become problematic only when they become *imbalanced*—when our fear tips into paralysis, when our anger tips into rage, when our sadness tips into despair. The key is to DEFEND ourselves against the forces that conspire to push us over that edge.

As you may remember from the story in chapter 2, when wolves were introduced to Yellowstone, the beavers must not have been thrilled. But it turned out that the arrival of a predator threat actually ended up *strengthening* the entire ecosystem. In the same way that vaccinations defend our body against disease by actually introducing a virus into our immune system, the introduction of threats into our Ecosystem of Potential can help us inoculate ourselves against them. Both are examples of how the presence of seemingly negative forces in your life can serve to make your system stronger and healthier. This chapter is about how to turn those negatives into sources of strength and resilience so you can thrive in a sometimes imbalanced world.

DEFENSE AGAINST THE DARK ARTS

When I was a graduate student at Harvard, I spent most of my time in coffee shops writing, thinking, and meeting people. But when I wanted a change of scenery, I would sample the different libraries on campus. Each one, from the law school library to the design school library, had not only a different look but also a different feel. I began to notice that every time I went to study in the Harvard Law School Library, I would leave feeling frustrated, irritated, and depleted—but for no reason. What could possibly be attacking my energy and focus in the Harvard law library that left me alone elsewhere?

A conversation with another grad student soon gave me my answer. She had been at Harvard for a while and was a certified connoisseur of study places on campus. Widener Library, where most undergrads studied, was, she informed me, "a pleasing mixture of youthful optimism and serious industry, with a mild reduction of inadequacy"—in other words, a good place for finding motivation on projects on which you were slacking. The Divinity School Library she described as "austere but with deep underlying notes and hints of inspiration"—that is, a good place for writing papers on expansive topics. The "velvety and cloying" libraries in the residential undergrad houses were good, she said, for emailing and making out. The law library, however, had "beautiful presentation, but with a spiky acidic palate with a bitter finish"—which she found was helpful for nothing. She was right. The law school was one of the two most beautiful libraries, but after a few visits, I avoided it like the plague. The reason why leads us back to the research at the heart of Big Potential.

In SURROUND we learned about how our brains are programmed for emotional and social contagion, and how the presence of even one positive person in a community can actually "infect" everyone in it with positivity. By the same token, research shows that we can also pick up negativity, stress, and apathy like secondhand smoke. Indeed, researchers Engert, Miller, Kirschbaum, and Singer have found that simply observing someone who is stressed—especially a coworker or family member—can have an immediate effect upon our own nervous systems, raising our levels of the stress hormone cortisol by as much as 26 percent. Yet, secondhand stress is almost as potent when it comes from a stranger; when observers watched a stressful event on video with strangers, 24 percent still showed a stress response.[1] Moreover, researchers Friedman and Riggio from UC Riverside found if someone in your visual field is anxious and highly expressive—either verbally or nonverbally—there's a high likelihood you'll experience those emotions as well.[2] Research has shown that even bankers on trading floors separated by glass walls can pick up the panic of a person across the room just by seeing their body language.

And incredibly, you don't even have to see or hear someone to pick up their stress; you can also smell it. New research shows that stress produces specific hormones that are released when we sweat.[3] And the human olfactory system can not only pick up on them but even detect whether these hormones were the result of low stress or high stress. In short, being surrounded by only negative and stressed-out people very quickly tips our balance from motivated and positive to frazzled and negative.

Notoriously one of the most hyper-competitive places at an already hyper-competitive university, Harvard Law School is a veritable petri dish of negativity, anxiety, frustration, and stress. In previous research, my colleague Liz Peterson found that while incoming law students have average levels of pessimism and depression, by month four those levels are triple the national average. Moreover, in contrast to the business school students, who famously meet weekly for mixers and social events, the law school students attend just two social events organized through the school each year, leading to more competition and less connection. Which is why, as you sit among the stacks of elegantly leather-bound law dictionaries and volumes of case law, you don't have to be studying for the bar exam to pick up the visual and olfactory assaults on your motivation and productivity. If we don't DEFEND strategically, just being in the same environment with people who are emanating competitiveness and stress can diminish our potential.

In SURROUND we talked about how, in today's world, we are hyper-exposed to other people for practically all our waking hours. We pick up on our coworkers' stressed-out energy all day in our open-plan offices. We constantly absorb depressing or anxiety-provoking news articles, or nasty or negative comments on social media. We viscerally feel the tense, urgent body language of people on subways, buses, and planes. These forces are inevitable and unescapable in our modern world. This is why it is crucial to not only find Positive Influencers to surround yourself with but also to DEFEND against the inevitable negative influences in your environment.

And unfortunately, there are more of them today than ever. Our news is heavily skewed negative.[4] Our stressors at work and school are at historic levels. Depression and anxiety rates have risen dramatically.[5] Moreover, it takes only a single negative in our life to imbalance the entire system. In *The Hidden Power of Social Networks*, the authors, Rob Cross and Andrew Parker, describe in-depth research suggesting that "roughly 90 percent of anxiety at work is created by 5 percent of one's network—the people who sap energy.[6] And Harvard Business School research shows that a single toxic person has a much greater impact than a superstar on a team.[7] We are starting to learn that these harmful forces can even be hidden, infiltrating our ecosystem without our knowing it.

So think of this chapter as being like a class on the Defense Against the Dark Arts (I've always wanted to write that). As any Harry Potter fan knows, it is great to have the power to work magic to defend against evil forces. I can't promise any magic, but I will offer five strategies for defending, disarming, and overcoming those forces that threaten our energy, creativity, passion, and potential:

STRATEGY #1: Build a moat.

STRATEGY #2: Build a mental stronghold.

STRATEGY #3: Learn the art of Mental Aikido.

STRATEGY #4: Take a vacation from your problems.

STRATEGY #5: Pick your battles.

Note that this is the shortest chapter but it is also the most strategy dense. I'm not suggesting that you try every single strategy in this chapter. Rather, find one that you feel you could put into practice effectively at work or with your family right now; if it works, add another one. Build your defenses strategically, one at a time, and build them fully before moving on to others. If you construct half a wall, invaders can just walk around it.

So let's begin with our first strategy: building a moat around our day to protect our mood, our optimism, and our energy from negativity attacks.

STRATEGY #1: BUILD A MOAT

Mont Saint-Michel is one of the most beautiful places in the world. After I graduated from college, I went to study French in Paris, where I failed to learn the language but mastered eating constantly. One weekend, I visited the island of Mont Saint-Michel, whose fortresses have since served as the inspiration for the castles in the movie *Tangled* and in the video game *Dark Souls* (which, by the way, I'm amazing at). During the Hundred Years' War a small group of soldiers stationed on the island was able to fend off a full-on attack by the much more powerful English. This was due not to the skill of their forces, superior planning, or dumb luck, but because the monastery and community sit on a "tidal island," which means that at all times except for the hours of low tide, it is surrounded by a moat created entirely by nature. This is not a puny, shallow little moat. This moat increases as much as forty-six feet between low tide and high! Each day, as the tides came in, the water would swallow up the small causeway to the island, rendering passage to the castle impossible, which meant that this small group of soldiers didn't have to defend against the British all day long; they had to rally their troops and their energy to fend off attacks only during the hours of low tide. A tidal moat is the perfect metaphor for the kind of moat I use in my everyday life.

We live in a society where technology allows us to be more interconnected than at any time in human history, and yet, as our mediums for connection have multiplied, our happiness has decreased. That's because we now have an unlimited, continually replenishing supply of negativity available instantly at our fingertips: everywhere from the news apps on our phones to the

Twitter feeds and Facebook pages we scroll constantly to the email in our inboxes—and many of us are addicted to it. Imagine trying to describe this phenomenon to someone living as recently as a century ago: *You'll never believe it—but in the future, you'll have the ability to instantly find out if something bad is going on anywhere in the world, anywhere, any time of the day. Yep! We have figured out a way for someone else to totally wreck your mood, concentration, and optimism with a finger stroke on your iPhone. . . . I'll explain what that is later.* Think about it. For the first time in human history, someone you don't know and will never meet can have an immediate negative impact upon your life.

Researchers of positive psychology have known for some time now that hearing negative news can have an instantaneous effect on your stress level, but new studies that Michelle Gielan and I conducted in partnership with Arianna Huffington show just how detrimental these effects can be to our motivation and potential. Indeed, we found that just a few minutes spent consuming negative news in the morning can affect the entire emotional trajectory of your day; our study[8] revealed that individuals **who watched just three minutes of negative news in the morning were** 27 percent more likely to **report their day as unhappy six to eight hours later**—it was like taking a poison pill each morning that made all of your efforts, energies, and interactions throughout the day more toxic.[9]

When your mood is toxic, your potential suffers. How? For one thing, a large body of research suggests that a negative mood impacts business outcomes; when faced with problem-solving tasks, negative people tire sooner, give up faster, and come up with fewer correct answers. Moreover, a barrage of negative news shows us a picture of the world that is frightening and in which our behavior does not matter. In psychology, this belief that our behavior is irrelevant in the face of challenges is called "learned helplessness," and it has been connected with low performance and a higher likelihood of depression.

After all, the vast majority of news stories focus our attention on problems in our world that we can do little or nothing about. We see the market dropping five hundred points, or a tsunami leveling a coastal city, or ISIS poised to attack, and we know that no matter what we wish we could do, we are powerless to change those outcomes. Yes, it's important to know what's going on in the world, but our exposure to disproportionately more negative news has an unintended consequence: less faith in our own ability to tackle not just the challenges in the world, but our own lives as well.

But it is not just the traditional news media; we are also receiving negative broadcasts in the form of stress-inducing emails from clients, a grumpy colleague on the phone, a tyrannical boss in a meeting, or a pessimistic friend on Facebook. Social media is like an always-on news channel, and the content doesn't even have to be negative for it to depress or upset us! It could be the pictures of your friends on their fabulous vacations while you are at work, toiling in a cubicle. It could be a post on Twitter that a friend just got married, while you are still searching for love. A LinkedIn update letting you know that a colleague just got a big promotion that you would have loved to have. Or smiling faces of your friends on Facebook holding up college acceptance letters while you haven't heard anything. We *want* to be happy for our friends, and when we are in a good mindset we generally are, but when our mental resources are low, we are much more vulnerable to toxic emotions like envy, bitterness, and resentment.

These threats are all around us. So we need a way to defend our castle.

One super-simple strategy is to build a moat in your daily routine. The simpler the better. Here is mine, and I highly recommend it: No media before breakfast or morning coffee, and no media after lying in bed. By "media" I mean news, email, and social media feeds—not on your computer, your phone, your television, or anywhere else. Like Mont Saint-Michel, this is a "tidal moat" that protects you at your most vulnerable times during the day. When you first wake up you are low-blood-sugar, groggy, and only half alert. As a result, you don't have your full resources at your disposal to defend against the onslaught of the negative. The same is true later in the evening; exposing yourself to negative news as your brain transitions from the day to sleep can tip it toward fear or anxiety as you try to sleep.

In fact, research shows that any kind of media—positive or negative—before bed can wake your brain back up and cost you as much as an hour of sleep on average per night.[10] This is why the National Sleep Foundation now recommends exactly the type of media moat I'm describing—namely, power down all technological media thirty minutes before attempting to sleep. In a study published in the prestigious journal *JAMA Pediatrics*, researchers led by Ben Carter found that if a child is exposed to the bright lights and sounds of a tablet or cellphone before bed, it disrupts their biorhythms and ability to quiet their brain enough for sleep.[11] Unfortunately, 72 percent of kids ages six to seventeen go to sleep with their phones. The smartphone has become the modern teddy bear, with a huge cost to our kids' energy, attention, and success at school.

What's great about the moat defense is that you can build it in seconds. You literally have to do nothing other than resist temptation. At first it may be hard to break the habit of checking your phone seconds upon waking and falling asleep with it in your hands, but trust me that the more you do it, the easier it gets. Habits are formed and broken through action.

Of course, building a moat doesn't make negative influences disappear; it just keeps them temporarily at bay, giving you time to build your defenses against them. So in addition to building a media-free moat around your day, try these three simple, research-supported strategies for defending yourself against the constant flow of negative news:

Turn Off Alerts

Try making your consumption of news an active choice, rather being a slave to your buzzing or beeping phone by turning off your alerts for one week. Shut off push notifications to your phone or email. Even when the news isn't negative, these alerts pull our attention away from the present moment and distract us from our work, time with our families and friends, or the few stolen minutes of quiet contemplation we need in order to refocus or recharge. As soon as you give in to that alert, you're risking drowning in what author John Zeratsky calls an "infinity pool"—constant, effectively infinite streams of information.[12] But out of sight is out of mind, so the fewer the alerts you receive, the fewer mental resources you'll have to spend resisting these distractions. Don't let the fear of missing out get the better of you; if there's anything really important happening, you'll hear about it soon enough.

Cancel the Noise

We live in a noisy world, and it seems to only be getting louder and louder. In *Before Happiness*, I wrote about how in the same way you might cancel the noise on a plane using headphones, you can cancel out all the negative chatter in your brain by practicing meditation. Or, if you drive or listen to the radio or podcasts on the way to work, try decreasing the noise in your life just by turning them off for the first five minutes of your commute.[13] When you do turn the radio or podcast back on, try to mute at least one set of commercials per show. It's hard to tune in to the signal of our own lives when we're bombarded by all the noise around us.

Do a Meeting Detox

Pointless meetings are a black hole of energy and productivity that plague many teams and companies. But how do we know which meetings are noise that we need to eliminate and which are actually productive and necessary? You could take a page from leaders at Dropbox who, in a brave move, decided to go cold turkey and eliminated all recurring meetings for a two-week period. Though they knew they could never stay on the wagon forever, this detox period allowed them to break the routine and objectively assess the value of each of the meetings before they added it back into their workday "diet." It was like giving up all sugars for a month to figure out which types you need for energy and fuel and which you can live without. Over the next two years, Dropbox's meetings got shorter and shorter in duration—and perceived by employees as more and more productive—despite the number of employees at the company having tripled.[14]

Create an Automatic Filter

John Stix is a Canadian entrepreneur who made his fortune in the telecom world. Like many parents, he was troubled by the awful things kids were exposed to online. Then he realized that while technology may have been the root of the problem, it could also be part of the solution. So he used his technical know-how and created a device called KidsWifi. It looks like a night-light that you plug into the wall, but it is in fact a high-tech router that uses sophisticated algorithms to monitor and filter out anything that is not kid-friendly on all nearby devices. If only we had something like this to filter negative news, so we could go on CNN.com and choose the ratio of negative to positive that we wanted, instead of having to sift through gruesome images and stories about wars, natural disasters, and other forms of human suffering to be knowledgeable. I hope someone reading this book will create this invention!

STRATEGY #2: BUILD A MENTAL STRONGHOLD

On June 12, 2016, a man diseased by the cancer of hate unleashed his fury upon a crowd at the Pulse nightclub in Orlando. The aftermath of this tragedy—one of the deadliest mass shootings in the nation's history—was as chaotic as it was heart-wrenching. In the darkest hours of night, dozens upon dozens of victims flooded into the city's only Level 1 trauma center, Orlando Health.

On such a horrific night, there was but one blessing—how prepared the staff at Orlando Health was for the unthinkable. These doctors and nurses knew how to respond in a crisis situation, having honed their skills over countless tragedies and accidents, not to mention years and years of education. They had crafted smoothly functioning admittance procedures, protocols to prevent unnecessary errors, and practices to keep the communication among providers, patients, and families flowing. But just as important, they were *mentally and emotionally prepared*, because they had developed a mental practice to help them remain calm, on task, and hopeful in the face of immeasurable stress and sadness.

Two years before the shooting, the leaders at Orlando Health became committed to training all of their medical providers and staff members with positive habit interventions. To kick off the initiative they invited me to do two training sessions for their entire organization, from nurses to administrators. They then engaged *Orange Frog* trainers, who created a social narrative at Orlando Health around the parable I described in chapter 4, "EXPAND." As a result, the senior staff committed to starting their meetings not by talking about administrative problems, a lack of resources, or emotional stresses. They would start with gratitude. That mental training—starting every meeting by talking about the things for which they were grateful—helped them build a fortress of mental resilience that they would call upon as they served the Pulse nightclub victims.

After the shooting, they called me and told me that the morning after the worst tragedy the community had seen, they bravely began their meeting with gratitude. Gratitude for having been put there to help, gratitude for the outpouring of love from across the country, gratitude for the shoulders to cry on. At a time when the stress, shock, and grief could have ripped them apart, gratitude kept them together. I invited the senior staff to make a video showing how these interventions helped them stay strong in the face of tragedy, as well as how the community rallied behind them and helped them rewrite the mental narrative of the shooting for their teams. If you go to positiveresearch .com, you can see this video and learn how to create similar meaningful narratives, in good times and unthinkable ones.

In the military, a stronghold is a place the losing side will retreat to when things get bad; a well-stocked area that has been tightly secured in case of attack. A mental stronghold is a practice that creates a stockpile of mental reserves you can always fall back on in challenging circumstances. **A daily practice of gratitude is one example of a mental stronghold.** Here are a few others you can create to defend yourself against stress, adversity, or sadness.

Prime for Optimism

When I'm having a terrible day, when I'm feeling particularly frustrated or down, I try to think of three good things that have happened over the past twenty-four hours. This practice not only primes my brain to begin processing the positive again, it provides much-needed mental reinforcements to deal with whatever the world is dishing out today.

Not only does priming the brain for optimism create a mental stronghold that improves your resilience, new research shows that you can help others be more productive by getting them to reflect on the good things going on in their life. In one creative experiment, researchers J. Chancellor from the University of Cambridge and K. Layous and S. Lyubomirsky from UC Riverside[15] conducted a six-week study at a company in Japan, wherein employees wore special sociometric name badges measuring their activities and interactions over the course of the workday. It turned out that the employees who were randomly assigned to recount three positive events each week not only demonstrated higher levels of happiness after six weeks, they actually had significantly more energy and got their various tasks done faster! By simply getting people to focus their brain for just ten minutes a week on the positives in their life, they were more invigorated, moved more, got more done, and, as a result, were able to leave work earlier.

You can try this with your family or team. Pick a day—like "Thankful Thursday"—and make a ritual of thinking about three positive things that happened over the past week.

Create a Power Lead

Research shows that the first comment in a conversation often predicts the outcome. So we need tools to help us neutralize the effects of a person who sets an angry, stressed, or combative tone for an interaction. As the brilliant researcher who also happens to be my wife suggested in *Broadcasting Happiness*, you can set the tone by creating a "power lead" to short-circuit a negative encounter.[16] Try not to start your phone calls with "I'm so swamped" or "What a week. Is it Friday yet?" Instead, start with a breath and say "It's great to talk to you," or "I'm so excited about our work together."

Similarly, instead of returning a harried coworker's stressed nonverbal expression with an equally stressed grimace of your own, return it with a smile or a nod of understanding. Likewise, every time someone asks "How are you?," try to resist the urge to complain and instead (as long as it's authentic) answer with something uplifting like "Today is going great" or "I can't believe how nice it is outside." This simple technique will give you the power to change the tenor of the conversation to positive before the person even has a chance to reach for default conversational topics such as stress, fatigue, or how they are counting the minutes until five o'clock.

Invest in Mindfulness

The most forward-looking companies are willing to take risks to achieve greatness. We have worked with organizations ready to make all kinds of risky financial investments—from banks willing to take on toxic assets to hedge funds willing to take $100 million gambles on failing companies—in the blink of an eye. But their leaders would still balk at the idea of asking their employees to invest two minutes a day in focusing on watching their breath go in and out. Amazingly, among the more than nine hundred talks Michelle and I have given at conferences, we have only *twice* heard a senior leader dare to mention the benefits of mindfulness.

"Work faster, do more with less" is the solution of myopic, risk-averse organizations. Truly forward-thinking leaders recognize that letting their employees slow down is actually one of the best strategies for creating a productive workforce. Aetna, one of the leading companies to successfully apply positive psychology practices in the workplace, has seen incredible results from a training program designed to teach employees how to center themselves through meditation and yoga.[17] Among the fifteen thousand or so workers (more than a quarter of the company) who have taken part, Aetna found an average gain of sixty-two minutes of productivity a week, which is an estimated $3,000-per-employee increase in productivity for the company each year!

And even that number probably *under*estimates the bottom line value of mindfulness, as it doesn't include the positive impacts of employee engagement on turnover, rehiring costs, retraining costs, customer service, or client-facing sales. My good friend Heidi Hanna, head of the American Institute of Stress, often says, "Stress is a credit card for energy; you're going to pay it back, but with interest." To that I would add the corollary that mindfulness is a credit card for resilience; the more you spend, the more rewards you get at the end of the month.

Lest you think I'm suggesting you take three hours out of your workday to sit cross-legged on a hard bench, chanting mantras, research shows that significant results from mindfulness training are achievable in just minutes a day. A fascinating pilot study that Amy Blankson from the Institute of Applied Positive Research ran with new Google hires (called "Nooglers," naturally) found that Nooglers who took part in a program that involved meditating for just *two minutes a day* and writing down gratitude in a journal enjoyed higher levels of engagement than those who did not. And if the thought of meditating is intimidating, or just "not your thing," try spending two minutes a day simply watching your breath go in and out and being present in your surroundings. If you want to be a forward-thinking professional, stop thinking about the future for a moment. Instead, sit down and practice being able to return to your mental stronghold in the here and now.

STRATEGY #3: LEARN THE ART OF MENTAL AIKIDO

Stressing about stress has become a national pastime. It's easy to see why we do this, but by making stress into the enemy, we are actually arming it. Research my team and I have done over the past few years found that perceiving stress as a threat dramatically *increases* its negative physical effects on the body and takes a toll on our creativity, productivity, and overall effectiveness. But surprisingly, rather than sap our potential, stress can actually fuel it.[18]

A study we did at investment bank UBS with Alia Crum from Stanford's Mind & Body Lab, and Peter Salovey, founder of the Yale Center for Emotional Intelligence, found that if a leader can create a positive mindset about stress on their team, framing it as a challenge instead of a threat, participants experience an 8 percent drop in the negative health effects and a corresponding 8 percent increase in productivity over the next three weeks.[19]

How do we reframe stress? Ali and her father, Thomas Crum, have developed an incredible technique. Both of them are versed in the martial art of Aikido, a form of fighting in which instead of attempting to block an attack you use its energy to redirect its momentum. They have transferred that martial art into a mental one. The key is to let go of trying to block or deny stress, and instead redirect it more positively.

You, too, can use Mental Aikido in your life. In order to redirect the momentum of stress from debilitating to enhancing, you first need to realize that embedded within every source of stress is meaning. Have you ever noticed that people in boring jobs that they don't care about never seem to feel stressed about their work? And have you ever wished you were one of them? I'm guessing you haven't. Even at its worst, stress is far better than disengagement or apathy. To be honest, I've never encountered a stress-free family, a stress-free marriage, or a stress-free life. That's because stress originally comes from meaning. And indeed, our study at Yale and UBS found that the negative effects of stress are much higher when we become separated from meaning.

Think about it this way: If I tell you that your inbox is overflowing with spam, you feel zero stress, right? Those emails can languish in your spam folder forever as far as you care. But if I tell you your inbox is overflowing with business leads or with emails from family and friends, you feel stressed. How will you ever manage to answer them all in a timely fashion? Likewise, if your child's best friend gets an F in math, you don't feel nearly as much stress as you would if that were your own kid. We stress about things only when we care about them. For example, if I am stressed about meeting the deadline for finishing a manuscript, I know it's only because I care so passionately about getting this book into readers' hands.

So if you notice yourself beginning to feel stressed about something, ask yourself, "Why does this matter?" Think about why you care. Write it down if you need to, and stick that piece of paper to your computer monitor or refrigerator as a constant reminder. I remember when I was a student, when my motivation to work on a paper or study for an exam would grind to a halt, I would remind myself why I cared about the subject, my grades, and learning, and I suddenly would have a burst of energy again. Your brain HATES wasting energy. So if it forgets why something is valuable or meaningful, it simply stops devoting valuable energy to it. Mental Aikido is all about redirecting that energy toward the things that give you meaning.

Once you reconnect with the meaning in your stress,

whether it's your kids' happiness, your reputation as a strong leader, or your commitment to a team, you not only put your priorities front and center, but you can now channel that energy productively. You'll find that same inbox is suddenly so much easier to deal with when you remember it's full of emails about the exciting new project you just started. Driving around like crazy to get your kids from soccer practices to dentist appointments is suddenly not as exhausting when you remember that it is an act of love. As Dr. Kelly McGonigal, author of *The Upside of Stress*, argues, "Chasing meaning is better for health than trying to avoid discomfort." Behind every stressor there lurks something you care about; you can either fight it, or you can use it as a source of energy and motivation.

Frame Challenges as Enhancing

I get calls from leaders all the time who tell me that their company is going through a lot of change and stress, which they "know" will lower their effectiveness, drive away top talent, and tear apart their teams. I usually counter this by telling them to think about the military, a place where stress and uncertainty are the status quo, and where employees are on-boarded not with a beach vacation but with boot camp. And yet, the employees of the U.S. military remain among the highest functioning, steadfast, and loyal of virtually any organization on the planet. That's because after centuries of practice, the military has learned that if you go through stress (1) with the right lens, and (2) alongside others, you can create meaningful narratives and social bonds that you will talk about for the rest of your life. Instead of seeing stress as a threat, the military culture derives pride from the shared resilience it creates. And this has nothing to do with the fact that they are soldiers; every company and team can turn stress into wellsprings of potential by looking at it as armor, rather than as a weapon of mass destruction.

When we feel stress in isolation, it can be devastating. But channeling that energy into making others better can cause the negative effects to dissipate. Two years ago, I did a documentary with HBO called *State of Play: Happiness,* in which we explored how to create a resilient social support system within a culture where it is difficult to talk about positive emotions, and in the midst of high stress.

During the first half of the documentary, we examined the NFL to see how people create happiness in an organization where the average career is 3.3 years long, there is fierce competition and a high potential of injury, and many assume you are too "tough" to talk about emotions. During the second half, we looked at the Navy SEALs, one of the most elite units of the military, where merely acknowledging one's emotions is virtually unthinkable, and where there is high potential not only of injury but also of death. In both cases, we found that the secret to their extraordinary levels of teamwork, engagement, and loyalty wasn't just the stress itself, but *the effort invested in helping each other overcome that stress.*

For example, Michael Strahan, former NFL defensive end for the New York Giants, told me that his highest-performing year came when he decided to focus on loving being on a team and supporting his teammates as they excelled, rather than worrying about whether he would get injured and have to retire. After hearing similar sentiments from SEALs and other NFL players alike, the lesson for companies and organizations was clear: We need to help our teams see stress as a group challenge, not an individual burden.

A year after that documentary aired, I had the opportunity to interview Habitat for Humanity CEO Jonathan Reckford to learn about how to build and sustain a culture where challenges are seen as motivating rather than defeating. He told me that thousands of people sign up as volunteers each year, driven by passion for the organization's mission and a hunger to create change in the world, much like with the military. And yet when the volunteers find out that there is all this red tape, or that there is a scarcity of resources, or that there are obstacles to achieving all the impact they want, as quickly as they want it, many get frustrated. They begin to feel like the organization and the system are getting in the way of their passion, and as a result they quit.

But some volunteers see the scarcity of resources not as a threat to their passion but as an exciting challenge that activates their potential: How do I make the most of these scarce resources? How do I get around the red tape and other obstacles? And better yet, how can I support all these like-minded people who are engaged in this challenge to create a better world? Reckford said his job as CEO is to inspire and train leaders and their teams to change their lens—to begin to see the stressors not as reasons to quit but as the fuel of teamwork and motivation.

So how can you use this in your life? First, if you find yourself in a stressful or high-stakes situation, ask yourself, "Who is here in the trenches with me?" You can always find someone who is sharing in your struggle, whether they are coworkers, fellow classmates, or even people you don't know personally but whom you might meet through your network or through a support group. Once you've reminded yourself that your burden isn't yours to carry alone, challenge yourself to do anything you can to help these people, rather than simply commiserate with them. This reframes the threat as an opportunity to strengthen your empathy muscle, as well as the bonds of your support system.

Second, pay attention to the way you talk about the stressful things in your life. When you get home, instead of describing your work responsibilities as annoying, frustrating, or overwhelming, talk about the opportunities they provide to build new relationships, learn new things, and raise your potential. Even if you don't really feel that way at first, the language you use will begin to slowly impact your attitude and perceptions, and those of the people around you. Ever notice that parents who are always grumbling about work have kids who moan and drag their heels about going to practice or doing their schoolwork? As parents (and in the workplace) we lead by example. Make sure your words and actions are helping your kids, your teams, and even yourself see challenges as something to embrace rather than avoid.

Reframe Failure

Another form of Mental Aikido involves changing how we frame the concept of failure. As with stress, many of us believe that failure is something to be avoided like the plague. But in fact failure, too, can be a source of energy and motivation, if framed properly. Stanford researcher Carol Dweck has done the pioneering work on how our mindset predicts our potential, particularly when it comes to success and failure. And many are familiar with her findings that children who see failure as a springboard for growth (growth mindset) are more resilient, less easily discouraged, and persevere longer and harder than children who see failure as devastating and as proof of their inherent lack of intelligence or talent (fixed mindset).

But less familiar are the findings of a fascinating new research project Dweck did with Kyla Haimovitz to look at how these mindsets are interconnected. It turned out that a fixed mindset may be more "contagious" than a growth mindset; specifically, they found that if a parent has a "failure as enhancing" mindset about the world, it doesn't necessarily predict that the child will.[20] However, if the parent has a "failure is debilitating" mindset, the child is significantly more likely to absorb it. In other words, the more you can learn to stop treating failure like an unwanted dinner guest, the better you can DEFEND both your own potential and that of those around you.

Let me qualify this argument: This approach is not an endorsement of deliberately creating stress, or trying to fail, in your work or life. In most jobs, and for most people in their personal lives as well, there is enough adversity that you do not need to artificially create it. Instead, this is about taking that stress you cannot intentionally avoid and redirecting its energy in a constructive way, by framing the stress as a challenge that activates your potential as you undergo the experience alongside people who support one another and share in the burden.

Caution: Beware of Negative Illusions

In October 2016, I was invited to give an evening talk at a retreat for Bank of America in Southern California. Since I knew many of the bankers were from New York and Chicago, meaning it was even later at night for them, I did my best to keep the crowd engaged—or at least awake. At first, everything seemed to be going great, until suddenly, toward the end of the talk, people started to seem distracted: Some started looking at their phones, others started whispering to one another, and so forth. I didn't know how to read it. Were they tired? Was I boring and losing them? Were they skeptics and whispering about how they didn't buy into my research? In that vulnerable and insecure moment, I decided it was all three. Determined to win them back, I extended my talk another fifteen minutes, during which time I worked in some material that always plays well with audiences, but that only seemed to make them more disconnected.

Eventually, I gave up. Defeated and deflated, I walked back to my hotel, where I found ALL of them at the lobby bar, huddled in front of the television. Turns out it was Game 7 of the World Series. The Chicago Cubs faced the Cleveland Indians, and Cleveland had just tied it up in the eighth inning. I hadn't struck out with my talk after all; they had just wanted to get out of there in time to witness this major moment in baseball history. I had completely misread the situation, and as a result I exacerbated the problem—and my own stress.

It's human nature to be a little bit self-centered—to believe that *we* are the cause of a problem, or the butt of a joke, or the reason that a roomful of baseball fans seem distracted on the night of the World Series deciding game. But often, our read of such situations is a negative illusion; we are incorrectly perceiving a threat that doesn't exist.

Be on the lookout for "negative illusions" in your life. Maybe that person at the party who you think is being rude is just shy. Maybe that colleague who you think is intentionally slacking off is depressed or struggling with something in their personal life. Maybe that new acquaintance who you think is snubbing you is actually intimidated by you. When you catch yourself reaching for the most pessimistic solution to explain someone's behavior, ask yourself if it's possible that something entirely different might be going on. Just opening up the possibility of another explanation will stop you from falling down the rabbit hole of rumination and allow you to redirect your mental resources toward something more productive.

STRATEGY #4: TAKE A VACATION FROM YOUR PROBLEMS

We are told from a very early age that we shouldn't avoid our problems. As a researcher, I disagree. You ABSOLUTELY should avoid your problems—at least, temporarily. **Contrary to popular misconceptions, taking time away from your problems may actually help you reap one of the greatest competitive advantages that exist today.**

I started this chapter with a story about one of my son's favorite movies, so why not end it with a reference to one of mine? In the '90s classic *What About Bob?* psychiatrist Dr. Leo Marvin (played by Richard Dreyfuss) is desperate to get his annoyingly persistent patient Bob Wiley (played by Bill Murray) out of his hair. So he writes him a prescription—not for medication, but for "a vacation from his problems." Naturally, the plan backfires as Bob decides to take his vacation at the same locale as Dr. Marvin, but comedy aside, Dr. Marvin's prescribed remedy has some fantastic scientific validity.

Over the past two years, I've been partnering with the U.S. Travel Association on their new initiative Project: Time Off, a robust examination of the business implications of taking time off from work.[21] According to U.S. Travel, Americans are taking less vacation time than at any point in the past four decades. One reason, according to Gary Oster, managing director of Project: Time Off, is Americans think that taking time off will negatively impact their manager's perception of them, thereby reducing their chances for a promotion or a raise. But in fact, research shows that the exact opposite is true. Taking your paid days off actually results in improved perception by your manager and increases the chances for a raise or a promotion. *According to our new research, people who take ALL of their vacation time have a 6.5 percent higher chance of getting a promotion or a raise than people who leave eleven or more days of paid time off on the table.*[22]

Four out of every ten employees say they are reluctant to take a vacation because they have a lot of work to do.[23] Yet, according to U.S. Travel's research, one of the top two benefits of taking time off is actually increased productivity. Plus, even if you *don't* take a vacation, you're still going to have a lot of work to do—but you'll get it done faster if you first take some time out to recharge your battery.

In *The Happiness Advantage*, I describe research that proves that when the brain is positive, productivity improves by 31 percent and sales by 37 percent. Creativity triples, and revenues can triple as well. And in a subsequent *Harvard Business Review* article that was based on a decade of research, I concluded that **"the greatest competitive advantage in the modern economy is a positive and engaged brain."**[24]

But there's just one catch. It stands to reason that taking a beach vacation, or touring the Italian countryside, or going to visit an old friend or loved one, would make for a much happier and more positive brain—but this isn't necessarily the case. In that article, I describe previous research from the Netherlands that showed that the *average* vacation yields no improvement in people's levels of energy or happiness upon returning.[25] *But* that was the AVERAGE vacation.

In a follow-up study of more than four hundred travelers from around the world, my colleague and vacation companion Michelle Gielan from the Institute for Applied Positive Research and I found that 94 percent of vacations *do* result in higher levels of happiness and energy *if you approach them in a smart way.* Specifically, we found that if you

1. plan a month in advance and prepare your coworkers for your time away (so that you aren't fielding their frantic emails),
2. go outside your city (the farther the better),
3. meet someone knowledgeable about the location who can help show you around, and
4. have the travel details set before departing (so you're not stressing yourself out trying to find last-minute plane tickets or accommodations),

your vacation *is* very likely to lead to greater happiness and energy, and, therefore, greater productivity, performance, and resilience at work.

And if that isn't enough to convince you, consider that taking time off essentially means an immediate pay raise! No research is necessary for this one, just simple math. If you work on salary and *don't* take your paid vacation days, you just take a voluntary pay cut per hour for the extra time you work.

So next time you find yourself feeling guilty about taking a vacation—thinking that it will be perceived as a lack of commitment, or that you just have too much work to do—remind yourself that scientifically, taking paid time off improves your productivity and performance, speeds up your career advancement, and, if approached correctly, makes you happier.

STRATEGY #5: PICK YOUR BATTLES

In *The Happiness Advantage*, I tell a story about an experiment that I took part in back in college. In the time since I wrote that book, the story has taken on new meaning to me in the context of new research on resilience that is key to understanding this strategy. So forgive me for telling it again here in brief. In exchange for a twenty-dollar stipend, I volunteered to participate in a study at Massachusetts General Hospital whose objective, I had been told, was to learn about how the elderly fall. Because one obviously cannot bring the elderly into a lab and ask them to fall on the floor repeatedly, the researchers were paying poor college students to do it.

When I arrived at the hospital, I was given reflectors to place on my knees and elbows and was asked to walk up and down a padded walkway—repeatedly—in the near pitch dark. With each jaunt down the walkway, one of four things would happen: Either the floor would drop out underneath me and I'd fall. Or the floor would slide out to the right and I'd fall. Or a cord attached to my right leg would be pulled taut and I'd fall. Can you spot the pattern? If none of these things happened, I was supposed to fall *on purpose* (I guess to simulate how the elderly *intentionally* fall?). If I sound bitter, I am. For the next THREE HOURS, I walked up and down the treacherous walkway *two hundred times.* True, the research assistant did come into the room on multiple occasions to ask if I would like to stop the experiment. I did, desperately. But I hadn't been paid my twenty dollars, which was a lot of money to me at the time, so despite the painful bruises that were beginning to emerge on every inch of my body, I kept going.

At the end of the experiment, the research assistant was joined by the professor, who wanted to debrief me. She told me that I had been tricked, and that this had actually been an experiment to test resilience in relationship to economic gain. Had I stopped at any point in the experiment I would have received the twenty dollars, but they were interested in seeing how long I would persevere. As it turned out, I had been the only volunteer foolish enough to persist for the full three hours.

These days, we hear a lot about the value of perseverance and grit, and indeed there is an enormous amount of research linking these traits to performance and success. But I retell this story here because I now view that incident as the perfect example of why perseverance and grit, while critically important, are not *always* the best course of action. After all, my stubborn determination to see the experiment through resulted in my falling almost two hundred times and wasting three precious hours—for the same reward as someone who fell once and then got to go home. In work and in life, when we repeatedly stumble and fall along a certain path, rather than dusting ourselves off and trying again (and again), it might be time to ask if we are simply on the wrong path.

I realize this advice probably goes against what you'd expect in a book on raising the limits of potential, but consider this: When we persist for too long at certain goals, as researchers Suzanne Segerstrom and Lise Nes found, it can, at times, come at the expense of our accomplishing others.[26] By persisting for three hours in the falling study, for example, I lost valuable time that I could have been putting toward my own studies. Similarly, if you were to follow up multiple times with a potential client who turned you down, you're probably passing up several other meetings that could have been fruitful. Or by continuing to date that negative person who doesn't want to change, you're missing out on the fruits of a positive relationship. And by continuing to sink all your creativity, time, and energy into a terrible job, you are depleting the mental resources you could be investing in finding a better one.

Quitters sometimes DO win. Defense, resilience, and grit are valuable, but only to a point. If you've tried all the strategies in this chapter and your situation hasn't improved, that is a good sign that you need to move on. Because the truth is that some circumstances are beyond repair, no matter how powerful our tools are. If you are being consistently disrespected and undervalued at work, you don't need greater defense; you need another job. If you are in an abusive relationship, you don't need to inoculate against stress; you need to get out. If you wake up every morning knowing that your career path isn't leading to your North Star, you don't need a vacation; you need to try another path. And don't wait. The deeper the trenches you dig in your life, the harder they are to climb out of.

So while it's great to stay optimistic, if you're truly unhappy and you have the means to change, don't be a hero. Is this you I'm describing? Be honest with yourself. Instead of fighting a losing battle until the bitter end, why not pick a winnable one instead?

Knowing when "to hold 'em or fold 'em" takes wisdom and self-awareness, which is why chapter 3, "SURROUND," is so important. There is no scientific study that will tell you when it's time to chart a new course. Your Positive Influencers, however, can help you see and pave the way forward. You can check in with your pillar friends for advice on whether you are seeing your path clearly. You can connect with your bridge friends to find new routes to similar goals. You can call upon your extender friends to scout ahead for you to see where those alternative paths might take you.

To achieve Big Potential, we *need* other people to both defend us from the darkness and guide us toward the light. And we need them to help us sustain our energy and motivation—to keep that light ignited. In the final strategy, you'll learn how to bring together the SEEDS of potential to create a Virtuous Cycle of collective momentum that will allow the Star System to shine even brighter.

CHAPTER 7

SUSTAIN THE GAINS

Creating Collective Momentum

Brian O'Connor is a fifth-grade social studies teacher in Chappaqua, New York. In a world where too many parents bemoan that their kids watch too much TV, O'Connor motivates his students in a surprising way . . . by making them watch TV.

Specifically, O'Connor has his fifth-grade classroom watch *CNN Heroes*, a show that profiles everyday heroes from many walks of life making all kinds of meaningful contributions to the world. After each episode, O'Connor has his students identify and write down the qualities in the heroes that they want to someday emulate in their own lives. Then he takes it a step further and has his kids actually write letters to the heroes, thanking them for their courage and inviting them to a "Skype party" with the class to celebrate them and their contributions. At first O'Connor thought none of the heroes would respond. But incredibly, after seven years, the walls of his classroom are covered with pictures of his kids Skyping with these extraordinary men and women.

Most incredible for O'Connor, however, is seeing the bursts of joy on his students' faces as they celebrate and cheer these heroes who are so deserving of their praise. O'Connor says, "You would have thought we were Skyping with Katy Perry. They're a celebrity to my kids, as they should be."[1] But here's the thing: In celebrating the heroes, the kids start becoming heroes themselves. By giving the students a vivid picture of what a meaningful future could look like, these heroes are inspiring them to build meaningful futures of their own. A normal teacher teaches about heroes. A superstar teacher puts his or her students on the path to becoming heroes.

Teachers like O'Connor possess a special form of magnetism. One of the most magical artifacts in nature is something called a ferromagnetic metal. In a normal metal, all of the electrons spin in random directions, thus canceling out any energy. But if a magnetic force comes in contact with the metal, a few of the electrons begin to spin in the same direction. The more electrons spin in one direction, the more other electrons join them, adding to their collective energy. This transforms an ordinary piece of metal into a powerful magnet. Teachers like Brian O'Connor are just like that magnet; **the more energy they channel in a positive direction, the more power they have to pull others along with them**.

In this chapter you'll learn how to become one of these magnets, pulling people toward you and helping them channel their energy toward their Big Potential.

Most people know that Isaac Newton's first law of motion states: *An object in motion stays in motion.* . . . So why is it often so hard to sustain our forward motion in professional settings?

If Newton's law is true, once we begin moving in the direction of our goals, wouldn't the momentum just keep propelling us effortlessly toward them?

To see why this is not necessarily the case, imagine you go to a conference, where you are pumped up by a new idea, a charismatic CEO, altruistic initiatives, or even a slightly awkward happiness speaker. You leave the convention hall energized and ready to take on the world with your team. Then you get back to your desk, and slowly but surely you begin to feel that energy drain from your body and brain, and your momentum slows to a painful crawl. Pretty soon you begin to resent the work and forget all about what had you so excited at the conference. As a result, your performance plummets. Without a motivating force to continue to push you forward, not only did you fail to stay in motion, you're now going the opposite direction.

The problem isn't that Newton's laws don't apply to the world of work. The problem is that I did not quote the first law of motion in its entirety. The real law, which no one except engineers and safety inspectors seems to know, states: Objects in motion will stay in motion *unless acted upon by an unbalanced force.* Without a positive force driving us to continue, we will slow down due to the friction of life and the unbalanced negative influences in our world.

Now imagine you get back to your desk after that same conference and an enthusiastic coworker asks to hear all about it. Excitedly, you begin to tell her about the things you learned and the new ideas you have and the great stories you heard while connecting with people over drinks. Suddenly, your brain is not only reliving those experiences and connecting them to the present, but you've just used what you learned at the conference to inspire someone else. You can feel how your energy is infectious as you see her eyes light up when she suggests that perhaps you work together on a new project inspired by one of the ideas you've just described. Now, suddenly, your own energy and momentum have multiplied.

The Boston University physics department's explanation of Newton's first law describes this phenomenon succinctly: "Work can be either positive or negative: If the force has a component in the same direction as the displacement of the object, the force is doing positive work. If the force has a component in the direction opposite to the displacement, the force does negative work."

In other words, without some force helping you SUSTAIN momentum toward your goals, inertia and the world will slow you down. But when pulled by a positive force, you can easily collect more and more energy and momentum to propel yourself forward—at the same time increasing your power to pull others along.

Once we realize that our energy is interconnected, we see that the more you create across your ecosystem, the more potential you will unlock. In this chapter, I will describe three practical strategies for channeling that collective energy in the direction of your goals:

> STRATEGY #1: Generate more positive energy by creating Tours of Meaning.
> STRATEGY #2: Use Vivid Direction to generate a path for that energy to flow.
> STRATEGY #3: Accelerate the momentum you have created through the power of celebration.

The first four paths have "SEEDed" the process of growth, but to SUSTAIN that growth, we must remind ourselves that

Big Potential is a moving target, not a destination. If we become complacent our potential slows to a crawl. This chapter will show you how to SUSTAIN the progress you have made thus far by creating a Virtuous Cycle of positive momentum that lifts the ceiling of potential higher and higher.

STRATEGY #1: CREATE TOURS OF MEANING

Sixty-two miles north of Washington, D.C., the legendary Camp David has historically functioned as a place where world leaders gather to talk through conflicts, overcome friction, and pool their energy to generate the momentum needed to solve some of the world's stickiest and most pressing problems. Camp David is only a twenty-five-minute helicopter ride from the White House, and recent presidents have used it to varying extents and in varying ways. Ronald and Nancy Reagan took advantage of its pristine silence and visited there when they needed to retreat from the noisy world and recharge. President Carter chose it as the site for the twelve-day secret peace negotiations between Israeli and Egyptian leaders that resulted in the signing of the historic (and aptly named) Camp David Accords. Some presidents barely visited it at all, including President Trump, who deems it "too rustic" compared to Mar-a-Lago. But others visited it quite often, like President George W. Bush, who spent 487 days there over the course of his two terms.[2] President Obama was the first president to host his staff there for a retreat and day of motivational speakers, which is why, in the spring of 2015, I was honored to get a call from the White House inviting me to give a talk there.

For some unknown reason, neither Air Force One nor Air Force Two was available that day to come to pick up Michelle and me, so we took an equally glamorous option: We rented a compact (but quite presidential) Honda Civic instead. (Not once did Michelle laugh at my repeated joke that it was our "Civic duty" to drive to Camp David.) If you Google Map "Camp David" and follow the directions, you will not find it; the directions that appear online are intentionally inaccurate. Instead, I was emailed a photocopy of a hand-drawn map. I cannot share any more details, except to say that if you do find the right path, you will likely think you're being led down it in order to be shot. That path took us a quarter mile down a narrow road marked only by increasingly terrifying signs: DO NOT ENTER. NOT A ROAD. YOU ARE TRESPASSING. TRESPASSER WILL FACE LIFE IN PRISON. TRES-PASSERS WILL BE SHOT. And, finally, YOU HAVE ENTERED A MILI-TARY BASE ILLEGALLY AND THE PUNISHMENT IS DEATH. Then, a hundred feet later, we were greeted by a small wooden sign that looked like a not-so-artistically-inclined eight-year-old made it during craft time that says, WELCOME TO CAMP DAVID. After our Civic was given full security clearance, our "contraband" (such as my iPhone) was confiscated and left with heavily armed soldiers at the guardhouse.

Once our identities had been verified (and probably double and triple verified), the mood lightened and a golf cart sporting a placard with our names on it (I may or may not have taken the placard home and may or may not have it sitting here on my desk as I write this), driven by a friendly soldier, arrived to ferry us to a beautiful chapel. That's where we waited nervously as we listened to the only other speaker of the day: Admiral William Henry McRaven, the leader of Joint Special Operations Command during Operation Neptune Spear, the mission that resulted in the death of Osama bin Laden, as well as about ten thousand other missions (literally). Upon conclusion of the toughest "opening act" I may ever follow, I gave my talk and then I opened the floor to discussion. What came out of that discussion goes to the very heart of this chapter.

The first important thing to realize about everyone sitting in that Camp David chapel—from the most senior staffers on down—is that each one of them was a temp worker. That is, unlike the vast majority of my talks, where most people in the audience believe that they will most likely have their job next year, everyone in that room knew that they were losing their job regardless of the outcome of the election. How could they sustain their momentum to get them to the finish line—to avoid checking out and redirecting all their energy toward figuring out "what's next"?

I could see that for many of them, staying motivated and focused had indeed become a struggle. So at first I tried the tack of reminding them of what an amazing job they had in the first place—pointing out how when any of them made a phone call, they got to say, "This is Bob calling from the White House." Then I tried to get them to remember how they had always dreamed about working at 1600 Pennsylvania Avenue, and how fortunate they were to have had that dream come true. Unfortunately, these efforts to inspire were met with marginal or no return.

One staffer then talked about how they all stared longingly at ordinary "civilians" leaving their offices at five or six P.M. on warm days to play on the National Mall between the Smithsonian museums, and felt green with envy knowing that they themselves would be at work until nine P.M. at the very earliest—then return at six the next morning. One of the staffers noted that in the midst of all the stress, workload, and political infighting, her job didn't seem quite so cool anymore. It seems that even at the White House you can lose what fuels you.

But then we stumbled upon something valuable. When I asked my audience what still *does* ignite that spark, another staffer raised her hand and talked about how much she loved giving tours of her venerable workplace to her friends or youth mentees. She described how, when she showed people around, pointing out the grand presidential portraits, walking through the pulsating hallways, showing them the elegant meeting rooms where historic treaties were signed, the things she loved about her job began to resurface in her brain.

As she talked, it was as if her eyes were opening again after being clenched shut to avoid getting pelted by the shrapnel of everyday stress. The moment she finished speaking, the atmosphere in the chapel immediately shifted. Suddenly, everyone was nodding their heads, and one after another people started chiming in about how giving tours transformed their own relationships to their work. Why? Because the act of describing what it was like to work mere meters away from the Oval Office, of showcasing the rich history of the building to visitors, allowed them to reconnect to the *meaning* in their work. Simply seeing the excitement and wonder in the guests' eyes reminded them of the incredible privilege of being there, and that wonder in the guests' eyes would be reflected back into their own.

It may be hard to believe that these extremely high-potential individuals would gain energy and joy from something as seemingly pedestrian (pun intended) as giving walking tours. After all, these people were decorated generals, staffers with the highest possible level of national security clearance, and top advisers to some of the most powerful people in the world—with everyday duties far, far more important than showing guests around the White House. How could people with responsibilities like these ever have lost sight of the meaning of their work? Because objects or people in motion don't stay in motion unless they are acted on by an unbalanced force.

Most of us do not work in a high-stakes environment like the White House, yet we all have sources of stress and friction threatening to dissipate our energy. Both at work and at home, it's all too easy to get too focused on the duties that we need to accomplish over the course of the day, forgetting that it's a blessing to have kids we need to shuttle places, a privilege to have a house to clean and a job to commute to. I'm not glossing over the stresses of these responsibilities; I'm pointing out that the more duties we have, the more meaning we need to find in them. **Meaning is that "unbalanced force" that keeps us going, especially in busy or stressful times.** And "Tours of Meaning" help us to sustain this momentum by connecting us—or reconnecting us—to the meaning in our work.

You don't have to work at high levels of national government, or even at high levels of your company, to reap the benefits of Tours of Meaning. Nor do these have to be literal tours, like the ones given at the White House. The key is simply to turn your "tours of duty" into "Tours of Meaning."

When someone asks what you do, it's so easy to give the "duty" answer: I'm an auditor; I look for problems in tax forms. I'm a researcher; I look for statistical patterns. I'm a train conductor; I just collect fares. And so on. When you talk this way, not only are you boring other people, you're boring your own brain. Who would feel energized going to a job that was "just" anything? Remember, as Yale researcher Amy Wrzesniewski argued, your engagement, success, and energy—and in turn your potential—are predicted by whether you think of your occupation as "just a job," or as a means to a paycheck, or a "calling," where there is meaning in your work.

I want you to rewrite that speech you tell people at cocktail parties when they ask you what you do. Move away from talking about your daily duties and toward talking about the larger meaning in your work. If you're a lawyer, your job is not "just" to write briefs and bill clients today, but rather to help families find justice, or to uphold the law. If you are a teacher, you're not "just" grading papers this week; you're helping educate a new generation of parents and leaders. If you're a sanitation worker, you are not "just" cleaning up the streets and parks; you're trying to protect the planet and give future generations a chance to know nature.

The very best way I have seen to reconnect with meaning is to create a visual narrative of it. For example, invite people on your team or in your family to send you photos of their most meaningful moments over the past year, and then "immortalize" them into a physical photo album or online photo book (there are tons of websites that make this an easy, fifteen-to-thirty-minute activity to do). Not only does the act of doing this meaningful activity provide you—and your team—with a shot of energy; it leaves you with a lasting "memento of meaning"—a source of fuel you can tap anytime you are running low. The Italian poet Cesare Pavese wrote, "We do not remember days, we remember moments." To this I would add that the more you revisit the memory of those meaningful moments, the more value you reap. Moreover, by involving others in the Tour of Meaning, you make this a source of collective momentum and energy.

One company that has figured out a good strategy for generating collective momentum is Zappos. I was once invited to an all-hands meeting at the online shoe and clothing shop, and when I landed at the airport, a call center employee who was to be my tour guide for the day came to pick me up. (It seemed that Air Force One and Two were busy that day also.)

Zappos, as many know, famously invites business leaders from around the world to tour their offices in order to learn about the magic of Zappos. But while those leaders leave with important lessons about creating a positive company culture, the *real* value of this tradition is brilliant and hidden, because these are, in fact, Tours of Meaning, whose value is actually to the Zappos employees. Just like the White House staffers, when they see small groups of important business leaders walking through their call center and marveling at their efficiency, getting infected by the positive energy, or asking questions about how to replicate Zappos's practices in their own companies, they are reminded just how lucky they are to work in a place with such an amazing culture.

Remember, Big Potential is about leveraging the power of others, and it is often easier for others to see meaning in our life than it is for us when we are in the thick of it. So recruit some meaning makers to help you see what you're missing. For example, my two-year-old son doesn't care much about research or science right now, but he loves garbage trucks. And I love him. So twice a week, we go out in the morning and stand in the alley hoping for a glimpse of his personal heroes. When we see the trash collectors come, he watches with fascination as they open can after can of smelly refuse. At first they seem to be going about their work as normal, but as soon as they notice Leo watching them with adoring eyes, you can see them smile. Suddenly, they start moving with more zeal and alacrity, and they often stop to compact the trash right in front of us, just to elicit the high-pitched cheers from a tiny fan. I like to think that

that extra energy stays with them as they turn off on another street, and then another, and maybe even when they return home to their own kids that day.

So when you talk about your job and your life to others, which tour are you taking them on? The one that depresses them and you, or the one that increases your energy and strengthens your connection to your work?

Remember, without an unbalanced force, people in motion don't always stay in motion. But energy alone is not enough to propel us toward Big Potential. If we want to sustain the momentum we have created, we also need a clear direction. Even if it takes you to unexpected places to find lasting meaning . . . like Vegas.

STRATEGY #2: UTILIZE VIVID DIRECTION

They say that what happens in Vegas stays in Vegas, which I hope isn't always true; otherwise it's very odd that companies would want to hold conferences for learning or motivation there. I was once there for a conference during which I listened to a CEO try to rouse his three thousand employees with vague platitudes such as "I know we can do it" and "We can achieve even more this year" and "The future is bright." As I looked out at the crowd of direction-starved attendees, it was clear they couldn't find anything in the CEO's words to latch onto. Instead, they listened blank faced and with just enough polite laughter and applause as is wise to give someone who ultimately decides your salary.

By the time the compliance officer made some brief remarks

(which essentially gave everyone a chance to catch up on their email), the energy in the room had drained completely, as brains began to turn off and tune out. Then a senior manager, not a member of the "all- important" C-suite, was given a scant fifteen minutes to speak.

Almost immediately, the energy in the room began to change as this straight-shooting, rather normal-looking senior manager came onstage and began to describe how he had been working with different departments across the organization to come up with a five-point plan for the next six months. This was the exact opposite of the CEO's "Profits could surge" speech in its level of specificity. For every point in the vision, the senior manager detailed exactly what the success would look like. Once we roll out X technology, this is how it will impact your processes, and these are the precise improvements you will see. By using Y strategy, we expect that these cities will start to show this type of gain, which we will use to generate media hits in a certain type of publication, thus raising sales in these specific categories. And when we succeed, this is what it will feel like when you get to interact with the delightfully surprised customers, and these are the kinds of comments people will post about you and our company on social media.

It was magnetic. I didn't even work there, and I could vividly picture in my mind how my engagement, my performance, and my results would improve as a result of these changes if I did. Despite the breakneck speed at which the manager had to talk in order to lay out all the precise details of his vision in just fifteen minutes, the applause afterward was thunderous.

Later in the day, I went to a cocktail reception. It was easy to get to the CEO to say hello, since he had only a few people circling around him, and even easier to approach the compliance officer, who, of course, was drinking alone. But I couldn't get anywhere near that senior manager, who was surrounded by swarms of appreciative colleagues who wanted to shake his hand and let him know how his speech had inspired them. It was clear that his brief talk had given them the shot of energy they needed to overcome the apathy and inertia I had witnessed earlier that morning.

In an age of hypercritical social media, some companies have fearfully turned toward hiring CEOs who are good politicians. They are deliberately ambiguous and sparing in details, too bland to cause a scandal, and too vague to pin a disagreement on. The problem with such executives is that they fail to inspire any sort of energy, motivation, or direction. But this manager clearly understood that the magic is in the details—that the difference between empty motivational platitudes and long-term, sustainable momentum starts with helping people visualize exactly what that "brighter future" could look like.

If you're a very literal-minded or pragmatic person, you might be coming to this section with a healthy dose of skepticism about the power of visualization. And indeed there are many who are not wrong to believe that visualizing success often amounts to little more than a lazy substitute for actually doing something to make that success happen. Yet, visualization is about much more than just sitting back and imagining that good things will happen. There is a huge body of research suggesting that mental imagery can dramatically impact our actions.

New research coming out of Oxford and Cambridge, for example, suggests that your ability to *vividly* imagine details about a bright future dramatically increases your energy and momentum, which leads, in turn, to constructive action. When our mind's eye can picture exactly what that future looks like, it can orient itself in the direction of the bright future we envision.[3]

This is largely because the more vividly we can picture something, the more attainable it feels. In a book that makes a boring sport less boring, *Golf My Way*, Jack Nicklaus, a golfing legend, describes his mental game in exacting detail. Note well how vivid the imagery is. It's not "I imagine the shot going in." Instead, he wrote,

> *I never hit a shot, not even in practice, without having a very sharp, in-focus picture of it in my head.* It's like a color movie. *[Emphasis mine.]* First, I see the ball where I want it to finish, nice and white and sitting up high on the bright green grass. Then the scene quickly changes and I "see" the ball going there: its path, trajectory, and shape, even its behavior on landing. Then there's sort of a fade-out, and the next scene shows me making the kind of swing that will turn the previous images into reality. Only at the end of this short, private, Hollywood spectacular do I select a club and step up to the ball.[4]

His is not just an eccentric ritual; there is actual data showing that visualizing a success makes it more likely to become reality. Research has found that if you visualize making a shot, your likelihood of making it goes up slightly.[5] More significant is that if you visualize waking up at five A.M. to practice, visualize practicing your form, and visualize the feel of the ball in your hands right before it leaves for the basket, your likelihood of making a shot rises even more. Similarly, I have found that when people with a fear of public speaking vividly visualize themselves from a third-person view (such as that of an audience member in the balcony) speaking competently and confidently, anxiety drops dramatically, resulting in a more confident and competent delivery.

These are what we call "perceptual simulations,"[6] and the full extent of their power has yet to be seen. For example, I am working with the Center for BrainHealth in Dallas to see how using virtual reality to envision a more positive future could have an impact on soldiers with PTSD or students who are struggling with autism or learning disorders. Building on research by Simon Blackwell and his team, who found that by increasing the vividness of our mental imagery of a positive future we might be able to help others move not only to a greater state of optimism, but also greater emotional and physical well-being,[7] we believe that by using virtual reality simulations—which is about as vivid as it gets—of positive social interactions or environments, the brain can actually learn to construct a hopeful image of the future.

Moreover, NYU researchers Tali Sharot and her colleagues published a study in one of the most prestigious academic journals, *Nature*, that revealed that the more detailed our visualization, the more we actually begin to *feel* the specific emotions of that future state at the neural level.[8] By envisioning the joy we'd feel upon getting that promotion, for example, we actually get to "pre-experience" that joy now. [9] And that, in turn, provides us with the motivation and direction we need to make that future happen. Vivid pictures are like magnets, pulling us toward that better future.

It is the vividness of visualization that changes behavior. As one example, the day before the 2004 U.S. presidential election, researchers did a brilliant study wherein they encouraged people to vividly visualize themselves voting from a third-person or bird's-eye view; the theory was that if people could "see" themselves walking into the voting booth, filling out the ballot, and so on, they would be more likely to actually do so.[10] And indeed, it turned out that the next day, those who had visualized themselves in this way actually did turn out to vote in greater numbers than a control group.

And incredibly, research coming out of the prestigious Cleveland Clinic suggests that merely visualizing healthy behaviors—such as exercise—can have effects similar to those of the behaviors themselves. Guang Yue compared people who went to the gym for a number of hours each week with people who spent an equal number of hours carrying out a vivid "virtual workout" in their heads. Not surprisingly, the ones who actually went to the gym had a 30 percent increase in muscle. What was surprising is that *those who had only a mental workout still had a 13.5 percent increase in muscle*—without lifting a single weight. And that was true for the next three months. It's clear that we have not yet fully tapped into the power of the brain when it comes to visualization.

Visualize Success Routes Instead of Escape Routes

I remember that back in college, when a girl I really liked broke up with me, my neuroscientist father tried to console me the best he could by saying, "Son, you just have a billion neurons pointing in the wrong direction." This was the oddest comment I have ever received after a breakup, but I now understand what he meant by it. I had gotten so good at imagining my ex with her new boyfriend—nuzzling together in a cozy corner of a romantic restaurant, making out passionately, or reveling in their blissful domesticity together at Target—that my brain had begun to believe that this version of the future was real. (It wasn't.)

Just as positive visualizations help us direct our energy toward positive outcomes, visualizing a negative future can stop our momentum in its tracks. This is why speaker and author Brené Brown warns her audiences against "dress-rehearsing tragedy," which she describes as mentally experiencing a theoretical future tragedy as if it were a real event. I've definitely been guilty of this. Sometimes as I go to sleep I think about what would happen if an intruder came into our house. Then I think about how they might try to attack Leo. Then I think about what objects I would grab to defend myself before rushing to his room. And then whether I would escape to the roof with him—but what if the roof was slippery? Would I try to jump to the ground while cradling Leo's head, risking breaking my legs and not being able to run further? . . . Just writing this, my heartbeat is elevated. My body is mentally rehearsing for this intruder. Yet, an intruder has never come into my house, and probably never will. And while there is value in taking some precautions in the event of such an unlikely occurrence, when we spend all of our time and mental resources imagining escape routes, we often fail to plan *success routes*.

Instead of playing out this nightmare scenario in my head, in other words, I could have fallen asleep thinking of fun things we could do as a family over the weekend, or new ways to teach Leo the alphabet tomorrow. That would have been a much more productive use of my time, and a much healthier direction in which to channel my mental energy.

Positive or negative, the more vivid the visualization, the more real it feels. And research shows that the more real it feels, the more likely it will impact our behavior.[11] **Only once we recognize this can we begin to move from a vicious cycle where**

our mental images feed our fear to a picture of the world that gives us power.

So instead of dress-rehearsing tragedy, why not try dress-rehearsing success? But just as no performer in a show can dress-rehearse alone, to create enough momentum to SUSTAIN the gains of Big Potential, we need to dress-rehearse success with our teams, friends, and families as well.

Pull with the Power of Story

Any good tennis player, or even an impressively mediocre one like me, knows that the key to winning is to first visualize where your shot is going, make good contact with the ball, then follow through fully. Yet too many leaders, including the CEO I saw in Vegas, have only a vague picture of where they want to take their companies or teams. Thus, they fail to connect with and inspire their employees, and then they fail to follow through, because they believe they have already failed. If the leader simply says "The future is bright" without providing any of the details, they are unlikely to connect with their team on an emotional level. As management guru Peter Senge wrote way back in 1990, "Vision without systems thinking ends up painting lovely pictures of the future with no deep understanding of the forces that must be mastered to move from here to there. . . . But systems thinking also needs the disciplines of building shared vision, mental models, team learning, and personal mastery to realize its potential."[12]

Business leaders, teachers, politicians, and parents wishing to build a shared vision, create mental models, and foster team learning can learn much from how the best authors use words to evoke vivid imagery in the collective minds of their readers. Simply saying "It was a dark and stormy day" is not nearly as powerful as describing how "the raindrops were drumming against the windowpane the way a concert pianist pounds on the keys."

If we want people to be excited about the direction we are taking them, we need to similarly elevate their collective vision of what a positive world can look like. For example, a manager might try to describe the effusive, gushing emails employees will receive from grateful clients upon the implementation of the new customer service training; a nonprofit leader might show pictures of smiling recipients while describing the potential impact of a new fundraising initiative; or a coach might describe the thunderous applause that will erupt in the bleachers once the team pushes through their losing streak to win the playoffs.

This is equally true for us as parents. A parent who simply says, "Think how proud you will make yourself if you excel at school" or "Imagine how happy you will be when you get into college" is not inspiring their child to excel nearly as much as the parent who paints a vivid picture of that child standing onstage giving the speech as valedictorian at high school graduation, or of going to their campus store to buy their first sweatshirt emblazoned with their new college logo, which they will wear to keep warm as they read on the benches outside the library in October. It's not enough to tell our children a bright future is possible; we need to help them envision how truly POSSIBLE that future could be.

I once had dinner in Milan the night before a talk with Martin Seligman, the father of positive psychology from the University of Pennsylvania, and Barry Schwartz, the author of the brilliant book *The Paradox of Choice*. At one point in the conversation (during which I was too nervous to utter a word),

Dr. Seligman stated these wise words: "Action is not driven by the past, but **pulled** by the **future**." To be honest, I didn't really agree at the time, but now I understand what he meant. We are magnetically drawn toward vivid pictures of the future.

One of the most effective and well-studied ways to vividly envision our future is to write about it. The act of consciously crafting your narrative of an event—past or future—directs our energy toward it. In one study, researcher Laura King found that when people wrote about their best possible self— the type of person they aspire to become and think is possible to become—their health and well-being significantly improved.[13] And in research done by Kristin Layous, Katherine Nelson, and Sonja Lyubomirsky, when individuals were invited to write once a week about the best future self they could imagine, after a month this simple act significantly elevated their physical well-being, happiness, and connectedness—the most crucial components of sustained potential.[14] So if you have goals you want to achieve, at work or in your personal life, write about them! And do it as vividly as possible. Think of it as writing a screenplay for a rich, Technicolor Hollywood blockbuster starring your best possible future self.

These techniques do more than just help us sustain the gains in the short term; there is lasting impact to our efforts to vividly conceive of a positive future. In one study of people suffering from clinical depression, not only did visualizing increasingly vivid images of the future increase optimism and lessen depression; those effects still endured a full seven months later.[15]

This finding is so crucial. I'm writing this in the wake of a tumultuous political election during which both sides claimed to not be able to envision anything but a disastrous next four to eight years if the other side won. While understandable, this outlook robs us of our energy—and only increases the likelihood that our fears will come to pass. Only once we can truly *see* ourselves overcoming whatever challenges we face can we sustain our efforts to help create a better world.

STRATEGY #3: CELEBRATE THE WINS

Earlier today, on a break from writing, I decided to take a walk around the neighborhood to clear my mind. One yard I passed had been decorated with posters and balloons, and on one of the car windows someone had written, in shoe polish, "Good luck at District!" with a soccer ball and other encouraging sentiments. I smiled. Something about it made me think fondly back to my high school varsity football days . . . or, more accurately, the days I spent binge-watching the TV series *Friday Night Lights*.

Whether we were the star quarterback or home on Friday nights watching television, high school was a challenging and confusing time for all of us. And yet while I can't say I miss the out-of-control hormones, the gossip, or the relationship drama, what I *do* miss is the sense of people cheering one another on through shared challenges and collectively celebrating the shared wins. After all, when was the last time someone put posters on your door saying "Good luck on your sales call!" or held a pep rally for you when you started a new job? The point is that it cannot be enough to just strive for Big Potential; we must also celebrate it.

If you rob life of celebration, you are not really living. If you have a success, at work or anywhere else, and you fail to celebrate with all those who helped make that success happen, that is not a win, because you've unconsciously bought into the Small Potential mindset that wins belong to only one person. We now know that Big Potential wins are collective wins, and thus worthy of our collective celebration.

Think back to the happiest, most memorable moments in your life. For most people, they have one thing in common: the presence of friends or loved ones. They are wedding celebrations, however big or small. They are birthday parties, and homecoming parties, and housewarming parties. They are holiday meals and baby showers and award ceremonies. For the book launch of both *The Happiness Advantage* and *Before Happiness*, my sister, Amy, baked cakes in the shape of open books and decorated them with orange and black frosting to look like the books' covers (of course, also adding a small mascarpone unicorn to mark her territory). If I'm being honest, a big part of why I'm writing this book is to get another one of those cakes. Celebrations are the ultimate motivating force, because they not only highlight a high moment in our life, they simultaneously ARE a high moment in and of themselves.

Early on in my studies at divinity school, I believed that the holiest people were the ones who sacrificed the most. After all, isn't freedom from material possessions one of the keys to living a saintly life? And the Bible is full of stories of people giving their earthly possessions away to the poor, or fasting for forty days in the wilderness. But the more I learned, the more I began to realize that in life, our feasts must be as sacred as our fasts. Fasts remind us that we need to be lean and focused and humble. Feasts remind us how much progress we've made and can act as fuel for our desire to keep striving for more.

Celebrate the Small

I once worked with a hospital in California where every time a cancer patient went into remission, a few of the nurses would celebrate by throwing a tea party. Soon the word got out, and other staffers and doctors asked to join. It wasn't long before former patients found out about these "remission parties" and they, too, wanted to occasionally attend as well. It makes sense; everyone wants to celebrate a big win, and cancer going into remission is about as big a win as one can get. But here's the thing. We need to celebrate not just big wins but small ones as well.

We often wait until something momentous happens—a new baby, a big promotion, a graduation—to really celebrate the people in our lives, and while these things absolutely should be celebrated, why should our celebrations be confined to relatively infrequent milestone events? In *The Happiness Advantage* I talk about how the two greatest motivators for achieving our goals are perception of progress and feeling like the finish line is close. There are going to be times, however, when the finish line might feel far away, which makes celebrating the small steps toward it that much more important.

My wife, Michelle, and I saw the power of celebrating small wins firsthand with one of our friends, who had started to become frustrated with how little her husband was helping out around the house. Both of them worked long days, and while she came home to cook dinner and take care of the kids, he would often just plop on the couch and zone out to ESPN. In the beginning she tried gently asking him to do a few things here and there, but it often took more work to cajole him than to just do it herself. The more frustrated she began to feel, the more she could see herself turning into a nag. She soon realized that she was channeling her energy in exactly the wrong direction; her nagging not only didn't motivate him, it got on his nerves, and so he burrowed deeper into the couch. This is a classic example of a vicious cycle.

Then Michelle suggested our friend launch a celebration campaign with her husband for one week. For one week, instead of nagging, our friend would actively praise him for all that he *was* doing to help around the house. (The key when you do this, we told her, is to keep the sarcasm out of your voice.) At first she thought we were crazy, but then she tried it out. Instead of mentioning the fact that the house was littered with his fishing gear and basketball clothes, she would say, "Wow, that was such a huge help, you playing with the kids tonight." Or instead of grumbling that he never helped with the cooking, she would say, "Thank you for ordering pizza. That was a great idea." For a full week, she kept reinforcing the idea that he was helpful.

You might wonder if all of this positive feedback might have made him feel like he was already doing enough and could afford to slack off. But quite the opposite happened. On Thursday that week he fixed a hose that had been leaking for two months. And on Saturday he cleared the table, which she said she couldn't remember him ever doing unless his mom was in town. Why? Because he was fulfilling the new self-image that his wife had given him. With his wife's help, he now saw himself as a helper, and helpers help.

Simply celebrating a person or a team for their companionship, their strengths, their everyday contributions—no matter how small or seemingly insignificant—reinforces a more empowered self-image and helps them see a vivid image of themselves as someone who is worthy of happiness and success. Likewise, celebrating someone for being kind, creative, or hardworking helps them see a vivid image of themselves as someone who is kind, creative, or hardworking. In doing so you become a magnet, helping to pull more and more of their energy in that direction.

You can try this approach with your boss, with your colleagues, or even with your kids. It worked with our son, Leo, who hates going to bed. At first our tactic was simply to be firm. But every time we said something like "Okay, you HAVE to get in your crib now," his response would be "Nope. Downstairs. Trucks." But once we started praising him for getting in bed and making celebratory breakfasts when he slept in his bed all night, everything changed. He now goes to bed willingly, because he's trying to live up to this image of himself as a good sleeper.

A fascinating study done by Adam Grant at Wharton Business School shows how celebrating the good in people can actually pull them in the direction of doing *more* good for the world. Specifically, he was looking at ways to turn people into givers.[16] One method, the one that most people thought would work, was to have the person take a moment to think of three times that other people had really given selflessly to THEM in the past. The idea was that reminding themselves of the generosity they'd received would make them want to give more—either "pay it forward" or "give back." This worked only marginally. But then researchers decided to flip it. They asked the participants to think of three ways THEY had been generous to OTHERS in the past. It turned out that the people who were asked to think of a time they themselves had been generous gave much more than the people in the first part of the study. Here's the reason. When participants remembered their past acts of compassion and generosity, they created a mental construct about themselves that they needed to justify, just as my friend's husband and my son did. In this case it was "I'm a giver. And givers give."

Thus, if you want to see Big Potential in action, why not pick someone in your ecosystem—whether at work or at home—and for one week, try letting go of what they are doing wrong and celebrate them for what they are doing right. One added benefit: It can feel good for you, too! As you'll remember from chapter 5, "ENHANCE," what the brain notices gets reinforced. So actively scanning for new things to celebrate about this other person will often shift the image YOU have of them. Now, instead of constantly seeing the things that drive you up the wall, you're reminding yourself of the best things about them.

Celebrate Strengths

Once you not only see people's strengths but celebrate them, incredible things start to occur. When four hundred employees on fifty-four work teams in Toyota's North American parts center went through a one-year program designed to celebrate their strengths and successes, productivity at the warehouse increased by 6 percent—quite a lot compared to the normal yearly variation around −1 percent to 1 percent. And the two teams who underwent a more intensive strength-based program saw a 9 percent productivity increase after only six months.[17]

In fact, a meta-analysis of sixty-five organizations found that those that celebrated strengths and successes showed not only more employee engagement but an average annual increase in productivity estimated to be worth more than $1,000 per employee. This means gains of more than $1 million a year for an organization with one thousand employees, and more than $5.4 million for the average company that participated in the study.

A study conducted at St. Lucie Medical Center in Florida suggests that these approaches also save companies money by reducing expensive turnover; after the seven hundred employees at the medical center underwent a two-year strength-based intervention, staff turnover dropped 50 percent—and the hospital's ranking for patient satisfaction increased 160 percent.[18]

Unfortunately, for many years, the focus of employee development at most companies was on people's weaknesses. Building upon what we talked about in chapter 5, "ENHANCE," managers would often pinpoint where their employees most needed to improve, and employees would receive training in those areas. The problem was, these approaches served mostly to reinforce problems, not fix them. Why? Because in showing people an image of themselves as someone to "be fixed," those managers were unwittingly pulling people's energy in exactly the wrong direction. Someone sent to a training on "presentation skills," for example, would begin to think of themselves as a terrible presenter, and unconsciously they would begin to act in ways that confirmed that self-image, and the desire to act in accordance with our self-image, or to avoid what psychologists call "cognitive dissonance," can be a force much more powerful than any set of skills learned in a one-day training session.

So it's no surprise that many companies are now focusing more on celebrating their employees, rather than "fixing" them. When I was creating the e-course on happiness for Oprah's OWN network, I invited the head of learning and development at McKinsey & Company to my home for an interview. Ashley Williams is one of the most innovative and effective leaders I've met in the corporate learning space, yet she is extremely humble and (as a true prism) always points her successes right back to her team. In our interview she told me about how McKinsey—known for being one of the most competitive companies—had found that their infamous "bash and build" style of performance reviews was consistently decreasing performance, increasing stress, and driving away good talent.

McKinsey prides itself on being data driven, so they set out to empirically test what type of performance conversations would have a better effect. And indeed, they found that diverting more energy and attention to strengths rather than weaknesses was significantly more effective in terms of client satisfaction, retention of talent, and partner engagement scores. The only problem was that the old style of doing things had become entrenched in the company culture, especially among the partners who had risen up the ranks through the "bash and build" mentality. So the company created videos of their most successful partners modeling how to focus the conversations on celebrating people's strengths. I love this for two reasons: First, that means that we really can change the old-guard mentality at an organization. And second, the videos are examples of how offering people a vivid image of what change can look like can help them see ways to celebrate wins, neatly tying these two strategies together!

You don't have to be a manager or work in HR to find ways to celebrate successes in your workplace. Anyone can organize a pizza lunch once a month to celebrate a team's collective accomplishments. Anyone can plan a happy hour outing at the end of a particularly busy week to celebrate how hard everyone has been working, or just because everyone needs it. The great thing about this strategy is that it's unbelievably easy to find reasons and ways to celebrate.

Celebrate Meaning

George Clooney, who owns a home in Lake Como, once said, "I think people in Italy live their lives better than we do. It's an older country, and they've learned to celebrate dinner and lunch, whereas we sort of eat as quickly as we can to get through it."[19] He has a point. Caught up in the busy whirlwind of work and life, we often forget to stop and celebrate the simple pleasure that good food provides. But to this I would add that we need to celebrate not just the food that gives sustenance to our bodies; we need to celebrate the meaning that feeds and sustains our soul and spirit as well.

After hearing a talk I gave to five thousand critical care nurses in Boston, Anne Weaver from UMass Memorial Medical Center found a way to celebrate meaning through all the trials and tribulations of working in a critical care area: She and three other nurses appointed themselves to a happiness committee. One of the committee's most brilliant inventions was a game they call "Celebrate You, Celebrate Me." The rules were simple: Every employee working in the critical care unit was invited to write down one meaningful thing about someone in the care area and one meaningful thing about themselves. For example, Anne might write, "Sharon took a few minutes out of the busy day to teach me something when I really needed her help. And I used humor to calm and comfort a scared parent." Then whoever was named the most times over the course of a month won $100 (which was to be donated to a local food bank).

Not only did this exercise bring the teams together; it also had another critical benefit. In those thirty seconds it took to participate, people were forced to think of something to celebrate about their colleagues *and* find something to celebrate about themselves. Because as important as it is to celebrate others' wins, we can't achieve Big Potential if we fail to celebrate our own.

Throughout the book we've been talking about how success

and potential are interconnected, and how helping those around us achieve more raises the limit on what we can achieve as well. But here's the thing. There's a reason they tell us to put our oxygen masks on first before helping anybody else in the event of an airplane crash. It's because if we aren't breathing in any oxygen, we're not going to be much use in helping anyone else. The same is true when it comes to Big Potential. If our own momentum is stopped or stalled, we don't stand a chance in helping other people accelerate theirs.

Celebration is the oxygen of Big Potential. And if we want to sustain the gains we have achieved, we need to keep breathing it in. We need to remember that whatever seat we sit in, we have the power to create change worth celebrating. The more we celebrate, the more we enrich our lives with meaning. And the more meaning we have in our lives, the more there is to celebrate. And thus we have created, and now SUSTAINed, yet another Virtuous Cycle.

CONCLUSION

All the Children Are Well

The hidden harmony is better than the obvious one.
—HERACLITUS OF EPHESUS, 500 B.C.

When Masai warriors of Kenya, some of the fiercest and most intelligent fighters in history, greet each other, they do not say, "How are you?" as we do in Western cultures. They say, "How are the children?" The proper answer, even for those without children, is "All the children are well."[1] That's because according to their social script, **things can't be fully good for one individual unless everyone in the community is thriving.** The science in this book proves they are right. We can't just worry about what is good for us; we need to worry about whether everyone around us is thriving.

I started my career at Harvard Divinity School studying Christian and Buddhist ethics. I was fascinated with learning about how our belief systems impact our actions. As I studied various religious traditions, it was clear that despite their differences, they were all wrestling with similar questions: *Why does selfishness get in the way of love? How do we find joy after loss or tragedy? What is the meaning of life?* Those existential questions that theologians, philosophers, and scholars grappled with three thousand years ago are the exact same ones we are still trying to answer today. In a sense, that seems frustrating. Have we really made so little progress in finding answers to these conundrums?

I see a similar frustration playing out in the modern world at the company, school, and individual level. I have met so many executives who are frustrated because they toiled for years to raise engagement at their company—only to see it subsequently nosedive. I have talked to so many people who are frustrated because they quite literally run themselves ragged trying to get their mile time below seven minutes, only to find that a few months later they are back up to a nine-minute mile. So many leaders at hospitals and nonprofits who are frustrated because they feel like every year they have to have the same conversations at the same conferences about how to overcome burnout and compassion fatigue. So many parents frustrated because they poured their hearts into giving their kids a loving childhood, only to be confused by the angst that suddenly takes hold when their children reach adolescence.

Is there no good solution for creating real and lasting change? Are we—as professionals, as parents, as ponderers of the mysteries of the universe—destined to forever keep spinning our wheels? No. Our frustration is born out of both a desire for something better and a misunderstanding of the fundamental nature of change.

If the past decade of research has taught me anything, it's that change is not a one-time event. You can't shower once and hope to remain clean next year. You can't exercise today hoping to never need to exercise again. In truth, we exercise today so we can move our body again tomorrow. We must always be on guard and repairing what breaks down over time.

Every individual, every culture, every company, every tribe needs not a one-time solution but a continual and constant championing of the positive. Stress and challenge are omnipresent in life; thus positive mindset, connection, and hope need to be equally ubiquitous.

Which is why change—like success, like potential, and like happiness—can't be pursued alone. Because true change, big or small, requires the support of champions who "get it." It requires resilience. It requires leadership, no matter what seat we sit in. And it requires collective momentum. None of which can be possible without the Ecosystem of Potential.

Yes, you, by definition, are the most important person in your universe. You are the center around which *your* world revolves. Which means if change is possible, it must *start* with you. But it doesn't end with you. At least, not you alone. You have to connect with others.

Only then can we make sure ALL the children are well, and not just today, but tomorrow, too.

If you have spent your life chasing Small Potential, you have been living, as Morpheus says in *The Matrix*, in a "world that has been pulled over your eyes." But now that your eyes are open to the power of Big Potential, I hope you will use it to find answers to your own pressing questions and create lasting positive change in your life and in the world.

In such a valuable and noble and lifelong pursuit, may the force *of others* be with you.

NOTES

CHAPTER 1: THE POWER OF HIDDEN CONNECTIONS

1. http://www.nytimes.com/1991/08/13/science/a-mystery-of-nature-mangroves-full-of-fireflies-blinking-in-unison.html.

2. Moiseff, A., & Copeland, J. (2010). Firefly synchrony: a behavioral strategy to reduce visual clutter. *Science* 329 (July 9): 181. doi:10.1126/science.1190421.

3. http://www.nytimes.com/1991/08/13/science/a-mystery-of-nature-mangroves-full-of-fireflies-blinking-in-unison.html.

4. http://www.reed.edu/biology/professors/srenn/pages/teaching/web_2008/mhlo_site/index.html.

5. http://mentalhealthtreatment.net/depression/signs-symptoms/.

6. http://www.aappublications.org/news/2017/05/04/PASSuicide050417.

CHAPTER 2: THE INVISIBLE CEILING OF POTENTIAL

1. Kester, E. (2012). *That Book About Harvard: Surviving the World's Most Famous University, One Embarrassment at a Time.* Naperville, Ill.: Sourcebooks.

2. http://www.nature.com/articles/srep01174.

3. Schnall, S., Harber, K. D., Stefanucci, J. K., & Proffitt, D. R. (2008). Social support and the perception of geographical slant. *Journal of Experimental Social Psychology* 44 (5): 1246–1255. doi:10.1016/j.jesp.2008.04.011.

4. https://www.nytimes.com/2016/02/28/magazine/what-google-learned-from-its-quest-to-build-the-perfect-team.html?smid=pl-share&_r=0.

5. Woolley, A. W., Chabris, C. F., Pentland, A., Hashmi, N., & Malone, T. W. (2010). Evidence for a collective intelligence factor in the performance of human groups. *Science* 330 (October 29): 686–688. doi:10.1126/science.1193147.

6. Fowler, J. H., & Nicholas, C. A. (2008). Dynamic spread of happiness in a large social network: Longitudinal analysis over 20 years in the Framingham Heart Study. *BMJ* 337: a2338.

7. From an online interview: https://www.reddit.com/r/science/comments/5wvz03/science_ama_series_this_is_dr_jenna_watling_neal/.

8. https://psychcentral.com/news/2017/04/01/are-personality-traits-contagious/118486.html.

9. http://factmyth.com/factoids/edison-never-invented-anything/.

10. Jung, D. I. (2001). Transformational and transactional leadership and their effects on creativity in groups. *Creativity Research Journal* 13 (2): 185–195.

11. Carman, K. G. (2003). Social influences and the private provision of public goods: Evidence from charitable contributions in the workplace. Stanford Institute for Economic Policy Research Discussion Paper 02-13 (January).

12. Leelawong, K., & Biswas, G. (2008). *International Journal of Artificial Intelligence in Education* 18 (3): 181–208.

13. http://ideas.time.com/2011/11/30/the-protege-effect/.

14. https://www.ted.com/talks/margaret_heffernan_why_it_s_time_to_forget_the_pecking_order_at_work.

15. Wilson, D. S. (2007). *Evolution for Everyone: How Darwin's Theory Can Change the Way We Think About Our Lives.* New York: Delacorte Press.

16. https://news.uns.purdue.edu/html4ever/2005/050802.Muir.behavior.html. In an interesting side note from someone who ate cage-free eggs thinking that solved most of the problems: When all

the chickens were cooped up there was only one territory so there was nothing to fight over, but when they were given free rein, it was a bloodbath because they fought for more territory.

17. https://evolution-institute.org/article/when-the-strong-outbreed-the-weak-an-interview-with-william-muir/.

18. https://www.nytimes.com/2016/02/28/magazine/what-google-learned-from-its-quest-to-build-the-perfect-team.html?smid=pl-share&_r=0.

19. Senge, P. M. (1990). *The Fifth Discipline: The Art and Practice of the Learning Organization.* New York: Doubleday/Currency.

CHAPTER 3: SURROUND YOURSELF WITH POSITIVE INFLUENCERS

1. http://www.deseretnews.com/article/695226634/Statistically-speaking-BYU-study-shows-assists-teamwork-important-to-winning-on-court.html.

2. https://www.forbes.com/2010/08/05/teams-teamwork-individuals-leadership-managing-collaboration.html.

3. http://www.businessinsider.com/teams-more-productive-than-individuals-2013-8.

4. https://www.fastcompany.com/3020561/why-women-collaborate-men-work-alone-and-everybodys-mad.

5. Cross, R., Rebele, R., & Grant, A. (2016). Collaborative Overload, *New York Times* (Jan–Feb).

6. http://money.cnn.com/2017/05/19/technology/ibm-work-at-home/index.html?iid=ob_homepage_tech_pool.

7. https://www.wsj.com/articles/ibm-a-pioneer-of-remote-work-calls-workers-back-to-the-office-1495108802?mg=id-wsj.

8. https://qz.com/924167/ibm-remote-work-pioneer-is-calling-thousands-of-employees-back-to-the-office/.

9. Smith, T. W., et al. (2013). Optimism and pessimism in social context: An interpersonal perspective on resilience and risk. *Journal of Research in Personality* 47: 553–562. doi:10.1016/j.jrp.2013.04.006.

10. Andersson, M. A. (2012). Identity crises in love and at work: Dispositional optimism as a durable personal resource. *Social Psychology Quarterly* 75: 290–309. doi:10.1177/0190272512451753; Heinonen, K., et al. (2006). Parents' optimism is related to their ratings of their children's behaviour. *European Journal of Personality* 20: 421–445. doi:10.1002/per.601.

11. Taylor, Z. E., Widaman, K. F., Robins, R. W., Jochem, R., Early, D. R., & Conger, R. D. (2012). Dispositional optimism: A psychological resource for Mexican-origin mothers experiencing economic stress. *Journal of Family Psychology* 26 (February): 133–139.

12. Duffy, R. D., Bott, E. M., Allan, B. A., & Torrey, C. L. (2013). Examining a model of life satisfaction among unemployed adults. *Journal of Counseling Psychology* 60 (1): 53–63.

13. https://hbr.org/2015/09/the-unexpected-influence-of-stories-told-at-work.

14. https://hbr.org/2017/03/teams-solve-problems-faster-when-theyre-more-cognitively-diverse.

15. https://hbr.org/2016/09/diverse-teams-feel-less-comfortable-and-thats-why-they-perform-better.

16. Granovetter, M. S. (1973). The strength of weak ties. *American Journal of Sociology* 78: 1360–1380.

17. Barabási, Albert-László. 2003. *Linked: How Everything Is Connected to Everything Else and What It Means for Business, Science, and Everyday Life.* New York: Plume.

18. https://hbr.org/2011/07/managing-yourself-a-smarter-way-to-network.

19. http://www.bmj.com/content/337/bmj.a2338.

20. https://hbr.org/2011/07/managing-yourself-a-smarter-way-to-network.

CHAPTER 4: EXPAND YOUR POWER

1. https://www.ted.com/talks/benjamin_zander_on_music_and_passion.

2. https://leaderchat.org/2009/03/17/leading-from-any-chair-in-the-organization/.

3. https://www2.deloitte.com/content/dam/Deloitte/ar/Documents/human-capital/arg_hc_global-human-capital-trends-2014_09062014%20(1).pdf.

4. https://www2.deloitte.com/content/dam/Deloitte/ar/Documents/human-capital/arg_hc_global-human-capital-trends-2014_09062014%20(1).pdf.

5. https://hbr.org/2016/04/culture-is-not-the-culprit.

6. http://www.securex.be/export/sites/default/.content/download-gallery/nl/brochures/Gallup-state-of-the-GlobalWorkplaceReport_20131.pdf.

7. http://www.securex.be/export/sites/default/.content/download-gallery/nl/brochures/Gallup-state-of-the-GlobalWorkplaceReport_20131.pdf.

8. https://hbr.org/2017/03/strategy-in-the-age-of-superabundant-capital.

9. https://txbbacareerservices.wordpress.com/2016/09/12/day-in-the-life-ali-allstate-leadership-development-program/.

10. https://txbbacareerservices.wordpress.com/2016/09/12/day-in-the-life-ali-allstate-leadership-development-program/.

11. Amar, A. D., Hentrich, C., & Hlupic, V. (2009). To be a better leader, give up authority. *Harvard Business Review* 87 (December): 22–24.

12. Amar, A. D., Hentrich, C., Bastani, B., & Hlupic, V. (2012). How managers succeed by letting employees lead. *Organizational Dynamics* 41 (1): 62–71.

13. http://www.huffingtonpost.com/entry/surgeon-general-happiness-vivek-murthy_us_564f857ee4b0d4093a57c8b0.

CHAPTER 5: ENHANCE YOUR RESOURCES

1. Hom, H., & Arbuckle, B. (1988). Mood induction effects upon goal setting and performance in young children. *Motivation and Emotion* 12 (2): 113.

2. https://hbr.org/2015/09/why-more-and-more-companies-are-ditching-performance-ratings.

3. https://qz.com/587811/stanford-professor-who-pioneered-praising-effort-sees-false-praise-everywhere/.

4. Meneghel, I., Salanova, M., & Martinez, I. (2016). *Journal of Happiness Studies* 17 (February): 239–255.

5. http://www.espn.com/college-football/story/_/id/18418243/alabama-crimson-tide-coach-nick-saban-teams-play-best-championship-games.

CHAPTER 6: DEFEND AGAINST NEGATIVE INFLUENCES

1. Engert, V., Plessow, F., Miller, R., Kirschbaum, C., & Singer, T. (2014). Cortisol increase in empathic stress is modulated by social closeness and observation modality. *Psychoneuroendocrinology* 7 (April): 192–201.

2. Friedman, H. S., & Riggio, R. E. (1981). Effect of individual differences in nonverbal expressiveness on transmission of emotion. *Jour-*

nal of Nonverbal Behavior 6 (2): 96–104. http://link.springer.com/article/10.1007%2FBF00987285?LI=true.

3. Dalton, P., Mauté, C., Jaén, C., & Wilson, T. Chemosignals of stress influence social judgments. *PLOS ONE* 8 (2013): e77144.

4. Gielan, M. (2015). *Broadcasting Happiness: The Science of Igniting and Sustaining Positive Change.* Dallas: BenBella Books.

5. http://www.independent.co.uk/life-style/health-and-families/features/teenage-mental-health-crisis-rates-of-depression-have-soared-in-the-past-25-years-a6894676.html.

6. https://hbr.org/2011/07/managing-yourself-a-smarter-way-to-network.

7. http://www.hbs.edu/faculty/Publication%20Files/16-057_d45c0b4f-fa19-49de-8f1b-4b12fe054fea.pdf.

8. http://www.huffingtonpost.com/entry/michelle-gielan-broadcasting-happiness_55d3b320e4b055a6dab1ee4b.

9. http://www.huffingtonpost.com/entry/michelle-gielan-broadcasting-happiness_us_55d3b320e4b055a6dab1ee4b.

10. https://sleep.org/articles/ways-technology-affects-sleep/.

11. http://jamanetwork.com/journals/jamapediatrics/article-abstract/2571467.

12. https://medium.com/time-dorks/distractions-are-a-nuisance-but-infinity-pools-are-the-real-problem-e84122d62c0c#.sjt2befmd.

13. http://www.amazon.com/Before-Happiness-Achieving-Spreading-Sustaining/dp/0770436730.

14. https://www.inc.com/rebecca-hinds-and-bob-sutton/dropbox-secret-for-saving-time-in-meetings.html.

15. Chancellor, J., Layous, K., & Lyubomirsky, S. (2014). Recalling positive events at work makes employees feel happier, move more, but interact less. *Journal of Happiness Studies* 16: 871–887.

16. http://www.amazon.com/Broadcasting-Happiness-Igniting-Sustaining-Positive/dp/1941631304.

17. https://hbr.org/2015/12/the-busier-you-are-the-more-you-need-mindfulness.

18. https://hbr.org/2016/06/resilience-is-about-how-you-recharge-not-how-you-endure.

19. Crum, A. J., Salovey, P., and Achor, S. (2013). Rethinking stress: The role of mindsets in determining the stress response. *Journal of Personality and Social Psychology* 104 (4): 716.

20. Haimovitz, K., & Dweck, C. (2016) Parents' views of failure predict children's fixed and growth intelligence mind-sets. *Psychological Science* 27 (6): 859–869. Article first published online April 25, 2016.

21. http://www.projecttimeoff.com.

22. www.projecttimeoff.com/resources.

23. www.projecttimeoff.com/resources.

24. Achor, S. (2012). Positive intelligence. *Harvard Business Review* (Jan–Feb). https://hbr.org/2012/01/positive-intelligence.

25. https://hbr.org/2014/02/when-a-vacation-reduces-stress-and-when-it-doesnt/.

26. Segerstrom, S. C., & Nes, L. S. (2006). When goals conflict but people prosper: The case of dispositional optimism. *Journal of Research in Personality* 40: 675–693. doi:10.1016/j.jrp.2005.08.001.

CHAPTER 7: SUSTAIN THE GAINS

1. http://www.cnn.com/2017/04/13/living/cnn-heroes-teaching-tool/index.html.

2. http://www.cbsnews.com/news/487-days-at-camp-david-for-bush/.

3. Holmes, E. A., James, E. L., Blackwell, S. E., & Hales, S. (2011). They flash upon that inward eye. *The Psychologist* 24: 340–343.

4. Nicklaus, J., & Bowden, K. (1974) *Golf My Way.* New York: Simon & Schuster. Quote first read on http://biovisualfocus.com/member/articles/where-the-focus-comes-from/.

5. http://psycnet.apa.org/psycinfo/1962-00248-001.

6. Moulton, S. T., & Kosslyn, S. M. (2009). Imagining predictions: Mental imagery as mental emulation. *Philosophical Transactions by the Royal Society B: Biological Sciences* 364: 1273–1280.

7. Blackwell, S. E., et al. Optimism and mental imagery: A possible cognitive marker to promote well-being? *Psychiatry Research* 206 (1): 56–61.

8. Sharot, T., Riccardi, A. M., Raio, C. M., & Phelps, E. A. (2007). Neural mechanisms mediating optimism bias. *Nature* 450: 102–105.

9. Stöber, J. (2000). Prospective cognitions in anxiety and depression: Replication and methodological extension. *Cognition & Emotion* 14: 725–729; Holmes, E. A., Lang, T. J., Moulds, M. L., & Steele, A. M. (2008). Prospective and positive mental imagery deficits in dysphoria. *Behaviour Research and Therapy* 46: 976–981.

10. Libby, L. K. (2007). Picture yourself at the polls: Visual perspective in mental imagery affects self-perception and behavior. *Psychological Science* 18: 199–203.

11. Mathews, A. (2013). Feels like the real thing: Imagery is both more realistic and emotional than verbal thought. *Cognition & Emotion* 27: 217–229; Holmes E. A., & Mathews, A. (2010). Mental imagery in emotion and emotional disorders. *Clinical Psychology Review* 30: 349–362. doi:10.1016/j.cpr.2010.01.001.

12. Senge, P. M. (1990). *The Fifth Discipline: The Art and Practice of the Learning Organization*. New York: Doubleday/Currency.

13. King, L. A. (2001). The health benefits of writing about life goals. *Personality and Social Psychology Bulletin* 27: 798–807.

14. Layous, K., Nelson, S. K., & Lyubomirsky, S. (2013). What is the optimal way to deliver a positive activity intervention? The case of writing about one's best possible selves. *Journal of Happiness Studies* 14 (2): 635. doi:10.1007/s10902-012-9346-2.

15. https://www.ncbi.nlm.nih.gov/pmc/articles/PMC5241224/.

16. https://www.amazon.com/Give-Take-Helping-Others-Success/dp/0143124986.

17. Clifton, D. O., & Harter, J. K. (2003). "Investing in Strengths." In *Positive Organizational Scholarship*, edited by Cameron, K. S., Dutton, J. E., & Quinn, R. E., 111–121. San Francisco: Berrett-Koehler; Connelly, J. (2002). All together now. *Gallup Management Journal* 2 (1): 13–18.

18. Black, B. (2001). The road to recovery. *Gallup Management Journal* 1: 10–12.

19. http://www.azquotes.com/quotes/topics/celebrate.html.

CONCLUSION: ALL THE CHILDREN ARE WELL

1. I first heard this in an interview with Michelle Obama. The statement was made by the interviewer Steve Pemberton. Confirmed here: http://www.worldcat.org/title/masai-of-africa/oclc/45890326.

INDEX

○ ○ ○ ○ ○

Also available from internationally bestselling author

SHAWN ACHOR

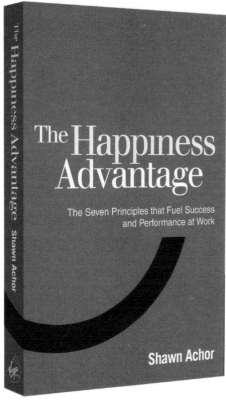

TED Talk with over 16 million views

A must-read for anyone trying to excel in a world of increasing workloads, stress, and negativity.

Happiness is not the belief that we don't need to change; it is the realization that we can.

Available wherever books are sold

Learn the five actionable tools for changing your lens to positive.

Happiness is a *choice*, happiness *spreads*, and happiness is an *advantage*. But before we can be happy or successful, we first need to develop the ability to see that positive change is possible.

Available wherever books are sold